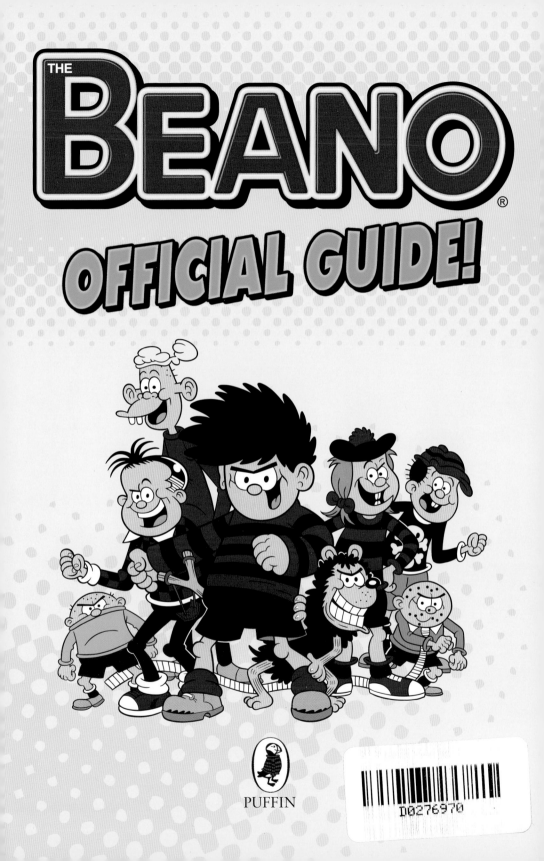

THE BEANO

OFFICIAL GUIDE!

PUFFIN

D0276970

CONTENTS

SQUELCH ME QUICK!

BELCH! BAARP!

WELCOME to Beanotown!

Greetings, and a very warm welcome from the Beanotown Official Travel, Tourism and Information centre (or BOTTI for short).

We hope you enjoy your stay in our charming and unique town, and that you're not just here because you're lost. Or your car broke down. Or you're on the run from the police and are looking for somewhere to hide.

A Trip Back To Old Beanotown

Beanotown hasn't always been the sophisticated metropolis you see before you today.

NOTABLE MOMENTS IN BEANOTOWN HISTORY

923AD
Vikings invade.

924AD
Vikings leave, as they think they might have left the oven on at home.

925AD
Vikings return (the oven wasn't on).

1605
The Funpowder Plot (a scheme in which various inhabitants of Beanotown plotted to have fun with a bag of sherbet).

1666
The Great Fire of Beanotown (allegedly started after an early Menace left a magnifying glass out in the sun).

It was first established over a thousand years ago, when a group of Vikings chased away the local tribe of Softans, then built the original Beanotown out of wood and bogeys. It's thought there wasn't much of a battle – the Vikings just coughed quite loudly and all the Softans ran away, never to be seen again.

1893

Beanotown homes get electricity for the first time! Ten minutes later, a distant ancestor of Calamity James electrocutes himself.

1985

Lightning strikes the Beanotown clock tower, stopping the clock. Everyone in the town is forced to have elevenses for two weeks while the clock is fixed.

PRESENT DAY

You are reading this sentence.

WHAT TO PACK FOR YOUR TRIP TO
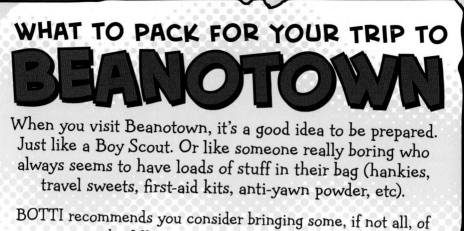
BEANOTOWN

When you visit Beanotown, it's a good idea to be prepared. Just like a Boy Scout. Or like someone really boring who always seems to have loads of stuff in their bag (hankies, travel sweets, first-aid kits, anti-yawn powder, etc).

BOTTI recommends you consider bringing some, if not all, of the following items along with you.

GROWN-UP ALARM

An essential piece of kit – in case you're having fun and a grown-up unexpectedly arrives to ruin everything.

SORE-TUMMY TABLETS

Just in case you eat anything made by Olive, the Dinner Lady at Bash Street School.

CHEWING GUM

Not just for keeping your breath fresh and minty, but also useful for filling in potholes and sticking things that have come un-stuck.

MENACE MINT
CHEWING GUM
CHEWING GUM

FASHIONABLE CLOTHING

To always look your best in Beanotown, why not try wearing red? Or black? Or a combination of black and red? Or red and black? The combinations are endless! Sort of.

Out on the TOWN

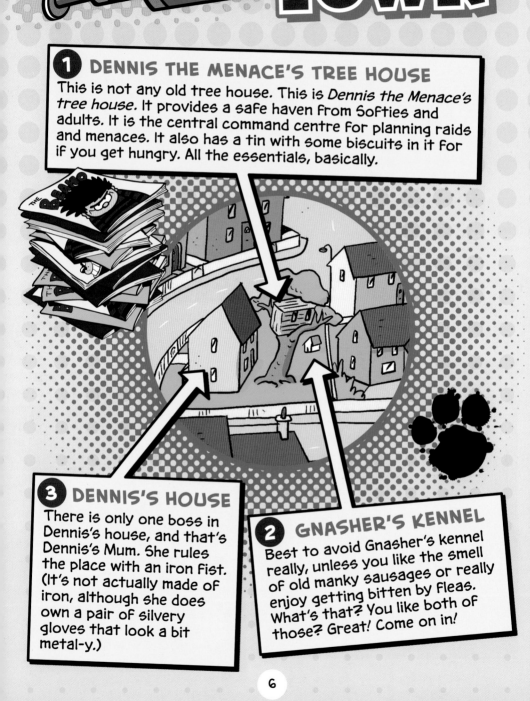

1 DENNIS THE MENACE'S TREE HOUSE

This is not any old tree house. This is *Dennis the Menace's tree house*. It provides a safe haven from Softies and adults. It is the central command centre for planning raids and menaces. It also has a tin with some biscuits in it for if you get hungry. All the essentials, basically.

3 DENNIS'S HOUSE

There is only one boss in Dennis's house, and that's Dennis's Mum. She rules the place with an iron fist. (It's not actually made of iron, although she does own a pair of silvery gloves that look a bit metal-y.)

2 GNASHER'S KENNEL

Best to avoid Gnasher's kennel really, unless you like the smell of old manky sausages or really enjoy getting bitten by fleas. What's that? You like both of those? Great! Come on in!

④ DENNIS'S GRAN'S HOUSE

Not just home to Dennis's Gran (who is the only adult who understands him) but also Gnipper, Gnasher's son and heir (well, someone has to inherit the fleas eventually).

FACT!
Beanotown holds the record for most pranks played in any town in the world. This is mainly down to Dennis.

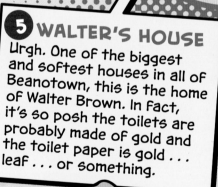

⑤ WALTER'S HOUSE

Urgh. One of the biggest and softest houses in all of Beanotown, this is the home of Walter Brown. In fact, it's so posh the toilets are probably made of gold and the toilet paper is gold . . . leaf . . . or something.

⑥ WALTER'S HEATED OUTDOOR POOL

You're not allowed to swim in here, so don't bother asking. That doesn't mean you can't still have fun with it, though. How about filling it with jelly? Or piranhas? Or jelly piranhas? Ooh, or maybe you could cover the entire pool with stretchy cling film so that, when Walter comes along and tries to dive in, he bounces right back out again.

DENNIS THE MENACE

NAME: Dennis the Menace, PhD in Menace-ology and Advanced Pranking.

AGE: 10

FAVOURITE COLOUR: Pink. Just kidding! It's red (and black).

PETS: Gnasher, though technically he's less of a 'pet' than a partner in crime.

HATES: Nits and wallies and, most of all, Softies.

LIKES: Skateboards, BMX bikes, catapults (and hitting things with catapults).

MENACE SCENE-DO NOT CROSS

Many people confuse Dennis's hair for his best friend Gnasher. They may look really similar, but there's a dead easy way to tell them apart. If it's carrying a sausage, it's Gnasher. Oh, and Dennis's hair doesn't have legs.

ITEMS COMMONLY FOUND IN DENNIS'S SCHOOLBAG:

● Massive extra-parpy whoopee cushion (for Mrs Creecher's chair)

● Hand-picked selection of fake bugs (for Mrs Creecher's glass)

● Map of the school's underground tunnels (for escape options)

● Enormous pickled onion and jam butty (for lunch)

Dennis wasn't so keen on his little sister, Bea, when she was born. But, when he saw she was almost as good at menacing as him, he bea-gan to really like her. Get it? BEA-gan? Bea? Oh, forget it.

ALL ABOUT DENNIS

Do you like to have fun? Then you'll like Dennis the Menace. He has many great skills, although grown-ups insist on not referring to them as 'skills' and always call them 'trouble' instead.

Need to menace up some stuff in your house? Just call Dennis. Need someone to play lead guitar in your band? Just call Dennis. Need to pull some pranks on some annoying people? Just call Dennis. Need a pepperoni pizza? Just call Dennis. Actually no, don't.

MENACE SCENE-DO NOT CROSS

GNASHER

GNASHER

NAME: Gnasher, aka The Sausage Nabber.

BREED: Abyssinian wire-haired tripe hound.

SHOE SIZE: Gnine and a half.

FAVOURITE COLOUR: Sausage brown.

PETS: A small family of fleas that live on his back.

HATES: Clean carpets. They must be ruined at all costs.

LIKES: Playing drums. And sausages. And playing the drums with sausages (although that makes them sound all wet and slappy, a bit like this: SLAP SLAP SLAPPY SLAP SLAPPY).

Sticky-up Ears
These finely-tuned lug holes can hear approaching Softies/teachers/sausages from several miles away.

Toothy Grin
The perfect equipment for a day's gnashing (or gnipping).

Skinny Legs
Gnasher doesn't shave them. Honest.

ALL ABOUT GNASHER

Gnasher is no ordinary tripe hound. He is also Dennis's right-paw dog, and father to Gnipper. He speaks Gnasherese (it's a little bit like Gnorwegian, with a little Gnigerian thrown in) and, because of this, only his closest friends and family can understand him. Instead of talking to him, it's better to just offer him some sausages. Everyone understands the international language of sausages.

GNIPPER

GNECESSARY GNASHER GNOWLEDGE

Gnipper has five sisters – Gnatasha, Gnaomi, Gnanette, Gnorah and Gnancy. He also has an Italian cousin called Gnocchi and a Mexican cousin called Gnacho.

Gnasher has the strongest teeth in Beanotown. He can bite through a metal fence (if you tell him it's protecting some sausages).

If Gnasher and Gnipper were to climb a tree and jump into the air, people would think they were a big raincloud and a little raincloud. They don't do this, though, because they can't see the point.

Gnasher and Gnipper's canine arch-enemy is Walter's pet poodle, Foo Foo. Once, Gnasher and Gnipper swapped Foo Foo's little pink bow with some bacon, and every single dog in Beanotown chased him round and round a lamp-post. Gnasher and Gnipper still chuckle about that to this day.

Wiry Hair
Cannot be styled (unless your choice of style is brush/hedgehog).

MENACING GEAR

If you want to be a proper Menace you need to be prepared at all times. If a good menacing opportunity comes up and you don't have the right equipment, you'll miss it! You wally! So here's what you should always have at hand . . .

CATAPULT

An essential bit of kit for menacing. Catapults can be used to fling all kinds of stuff at all kinds of people. Plus, the elastic makes a really satisfying *TWANG* sound when you pull it back and let it go. *TWAAAAAANG!* Of course, for your catapult to do any decent menacing, you'll need plenty of ammo . . .

TOMATOES

The classic choice for ammunition, the tomato is the perfect size and shape to be launched from your catapult. It's almost as if it was designed for this purpose (let's face it – it certainly wasn't designed for yucky salads). To cause maximum mischief, get an extra-squishy one.

EGGS

Can be tricky to fire from a catapult. If you get it wrong you'll end up with egg all over your face (and arms and shoulders). Instead, put an egg on a chair and, when someone sits down and crushes it, be sure to shout, 'You are the worst chicken ever'. Then run away. Fast.

PEA-SHOOTER

The perfect thing for shooting peas at people. Aim for the back of the leg if you want your victim to think they've been stung by a bee. Or, if they don't like peas, why not try aiming for their dinner?

THWACK!

FAKE SNAKES

As the old saying goes, a day not spent dropping a fake snake on someone's lap or shoulder to make them run around screaming is a day wasted. You wouldn't want to waste a day, would you?

FLEA POWDER

Put a bit of flea powder on a bed or couch and your victim will be scratching for hours! Or you could save money and just disguise Gnasher as a pillow or cushion (get him to tuck his legs in) and use his free fleas!

STICKY TAPE

This has more uses than just repairing leaky Beanotown pipes – it has many menacing functions too! Sticky-tape a note (e.g. 'I am a big Softy') to someone's back, or stretch some tape across a doorway so that when they walk into a room they get stuck there FOREVER. You can even roll it up into little balls and use it as emergency pea-shooter ammo.

TOP-SECRET Blueprints

BANANA-NANA GUN:
FIRES BANANA SKINS AT SOFTIES. ALSO HAS A
LOUDSPEAKER THAT PLAYS THE VOICE OF MY
GRAN TELLING ME OFF FOR CHUCKING BANANA
SKINS AROUND. DOUBLE THE THREAT!

REAR-VIEW MIRROR:
FOR SPOTTING ANY GROWN-UPS TRYING TO
SNEAK UP FROM BEHIND. GET THEM WITH
BANANA-NANA GUN (SEE BELOW).

HOMEWORK MASHER:
PUT BORING OLD HOMEWORK INTO THE
MASHER AND SECONDS LATER OUT WILL
COME SOME SOGGY, MASHED-UP BALLS OF
PAPER (FOR CHUCKING AT GROWN UPS AND/
OR WALTER).

TOXIC TOOTER:
CLEAR THE ROAD/PAVEMENT/ENTIRE TOWN WITH
THIS TOOTER WHICH EMITS A SPECIAL NOISE AND
SMELL (LIKE THE TROUSER-COUGHS OR MIGHTY
BUM-BURPS OF SOMEONE WHO HAS BEEN EATING
NOTHING BUT CABBAGE FOR A MONTH).

SAUSAGE EXHAUST:
PROPELS LINKS OF PORKY DELIGHT STRAIGHT
INTO GNASHER'S MOUTH. SPEEDY SAUSAGE
SNACKING AT ITS FINEST.

30,000 HORSEPOWER ENGINE:
NO HORSES WERE HARMED IN THE
MAKING OF THIS POWERFUL ENGINE
(ALTHOUGH A FEW WERE STARTLED
WHEN THE ENGINE BACKFIRED).

TAKING CARE OF YOUR TREE HOUSE

A good tree house is essential for planning all kinds of menaces, pranks and jokes. Here's what you need to know!

WHERE TO BUILD YOUR TREE HOUSE

DON'T build your tree house on railway tracks. Trees don't usually grow on railway tracks anyway. It'll get knocked down every hour by the express train to Beanotown-on-Sea.

DO build it in a tree with a good view of the back door of your house. That way, you can see your parents coming and prepare yourself to say, 'NO' (or, occasionally, 'yeah, in a bit').

DANGER!

FACT!
This year the Beanotown scarecrow received a pay rise, because he was outstanding in his field.

16

THINGS TO KEEP IN YOUR TREE HOUSE

☐ **SPARE CATAPULT AND PLENTY OF AMMO:** to fend off unwelcome visitors.

☐ **BISCUITS:** in case your tree house is under siege and you can't come down (and you get hungry).

☐ **A WHITE SHEET:** in case it gets chilly (or you need to pretend to be a ghost).

☐ **BINOCULARS:** for spotting long-distance Softies.

ESSENTIAL TREE HOUSE RULES
IGNORE THESE AT YOUR PERIL!

1 No adults. Ever. No matter how much they plead, beg or try to bribe you with sweets, don't let them in. Even if they dress up as someone famous and say, 'I'm that celebrity from off of that thing you like and I want to see your treehouse please!' Especially not then.

2 Have a password. That way, you can make sure only certain people get in: those who know the password, or those who are really, really good at guessing passwords.

3 No animals bigger than Gnasher. A dog the size of Gnasher is fine in a tree house, but a cow or elephant would be a disaster (they'd probably smell quite bad and may topple the tree).

Dennis's Favourite Pranks

MAKE DAD FOAMING MAD

Use one dad (who should be asleep).

Put some of his shaving foam on his hands, then tickle his nose.

When he wakes up he'll touch his face, covering it with shaving foam. Take that, Dad!

WORM YOGHURT

NICE CUP OF EEEEEWWWW!

Switch the contents of the sugar container with some salt.

Next time your parents put sugar in their tea they'll get a salty surprise!

FACT!
Early roads in Beanotown were made of toast, in the hope of coping with the traffic jam.

MENACING HOUR

Set all the clocks in your house back one hour.

Laugh heartily as the adults are late for work and everyone misses their favourite TV shows.

Then you get no pocket money for the next six months. OK, maybe this one isn't so great.

YOU MUST BE... JOE KING!

How many skunks does it take to stink up a room?

A phew!

MENACE FAMILY TREE

LORD PERCY MENACE
A famous poet of his time, Lord Percy published a book of his works called *Cheese That I Have Cut*, followed by the popular sequel *Here Comes the Thunder*. It's said Lord Percy Menace once farted so loudly while standing behind King George III that the shocked ruler's crown fell off and landed in his swan soup. Percy mysteriously disappeared without trace shortly after.

FLORENCE MENACE
Credited with founding modern nursing, Florence was given the nickname 'The Lady with the Lamp' after her habit of checking on patients at night with a lantern – she then used the flame from the lamp to light her bum-burps, much to everyone's amusement.

VINCENT VAN MENACE
A painter who moved to Britain from the Netherlands. Sadly, Vincent van Menace never achieved much popularity while he was alive, partly due to the fact that all he ever painted was pictures of underpants. That and the fact that he used to throw stink bombs at art critics.

DAME BARBARA MENACE

A writer of soppy romantic books (double urgh), Barbara Menace was an incredibly popular author. Her best-selling novels included *The Perfect Husband (to Throw Tomatoes At)*, *Never Laugh at Love or Farts* and *Love Is Dangerous but Not as Dangerous as the Tiger That's in the Living Room AHHHHHH!*

GRAN MENACE

Dennis' and Bea's grandmother enjoys motorbikes and seeing that Dennis has turned out just like his dad. She is one of the few people in Beantown who truly understands Dennis, probably because she's used to this kind of thing from her own son.

DAD MENACE

Dennis's dad blames his balding head on his son's relentless menacing, and blames his loss of smell on Bea's relentless farting. When he was young, he was as big a Menace as Dennis - but don't let anyone else know . . .

MUM MENACE

Dennis's long-suffering mum has more patience (patients) than a hospital, due to her son's never-ending menaces and pranks. She clearly loves her son though - perhaps she sees something of her husband in him? Or she likes being stressed out all the time.

DENNIS (THE) MENACE

The scourge of Softies and adults everywhere, Dennis uses a wide range of pranks and weaponry to cause maximum chaos and mayhem across Beanotown. Dennis once made a stink bomb so strong a tree fell over. And trees don't have noses, so how does that work?

BEA MENACE

The latest addition to the Menace clan, Bea has proved she is as good at troublemaking as her brother, after being voted the naughtiest baby in Beanotown when she was only a week old. In fact you can often hear Dennis's Mum shouting, 'Bea! No!' when she's done something naughty.

Dennis's Guide to . . .
Baby Bea's Bottom-Burps

My sister, Bea, is not just a Menace-in-training. She's also known for the room-clearing, nose-burning pant-blasts she produces. Such an impressive human stink bomb, at such a young age! I think she'll go far in this world. Here's a guide to some of the guffs she has in her arsenal.

SILENT BUT VIOLENT

Bea doesn't make a sound for these – not a rumble or a squeak or a pop. You only know she's guffed when you smell it. Then have to run outside to take big gasps of fresh air.

THE JACUZZI

A bath-time favourite for Bea. This pump makes the water bubble up around her and she can't stop laughing. Then Mum has to open a window.

FARTY FIREWORKS

A load of quick, short parps like a bunch of bangers going off. The fart of choice for Bumfire Night!

WHERE'S THE DUCK?

This bum—burp sounds exactly like the quack of a duck. Once I even convinced Mum and Dad that it was a duck and not Bea. That lasted for all of three seconds . . . until they smelt it.

RUSTY CAR DOOR

Bea did this when Dad opened the door of his car. She made a loud creaky sound, and Dad thought the door had gone rusty and needed oil. Then he sniffed the air and knew it wasn't the car.

RUMBLE IN THE JUNGLE

Bea first did this fart while visiting a zoo. The long, loud rumble made all the monkeys hold their noses and run away. Some even had to put bananas up their nostrils to try and stop the smell!

An Introduction
to the Study of
Little Squelchy Things

By Alexander Lemming SqD,
Professor in Wobbleology & Squidgetronomy

Greetings! Professor Alexander Lemming here, and I'd like to tell you all about the Squelchy Things.

What are these Squelchy Things, you ask? It's a good question, as you probably haven't noticed them until now – mostly because they live underground, and also partly because you're not looking for them. But that's about to change! Soon you'll start seeing them all over the place. So be careful where you step!

The Squelchy Things were first unleashed by accident, when Calamity James poured water over them, thinking they were Sea Monkeys. WELL, THEY WEREN'T. They were Squelchy Things: the fastest-mutating life form on the planet. HUZZAH!

LITTLE SQUELCHY THINGS

There's loads of them ('loads' is the proper, scientific term for 'jillions') and with my help you'll learn all about them. Ahem, let me begin . . .

Squelchology

Part 1

A COMMON LITTLE SQUELCHY THING

SQUELCH!

This is the most common kind of Squelchy Thing, but if you see one don't let that put you off – it's just as squelchy, wobbly and sloshy as the rest of them. In fact, my research suggests that the Common Little Squelchy Thing is up to 10 per cent more jiggly than the others (especially when it hears a song it likes).

A LITTLE BESPECTACLED SQUELCHY THING

You can spot a Little Bespectacled Squelchy Thing by its thick glasses and squidgy, squashy squint. The Little Bespectacled Squelchy Thing has clearly spent too much time staring at some particularly squishy books and, as a result, needs to wear glasses. This is because, unlike the rest of us, Squelchy Things aren't meant to read books. They are meant to wobble and slosh around. Obviously!

8 PLUG'S HOUSE

Alas, Plug and his family were banished from the Bash Street Flats because the other residents refused to share a lift with them. On the bright side, the Plugsleys now have a whole new bunch of neighbours to terrify with their hideous faces.

9 LES PRETEND'S HOUSE

The Pretend household is noted for its sparkling clean wheelie bins. This is mainly because Les makes a massive fuss whenever his parents try to chuck anything out. There is nothing he can't re-use for a pretend! He even pretended to be a massive microwave spag-bol meal once. Messy.

7 MINNIE THE MINX'S HOUSE

Stay out! There's a Minx about!

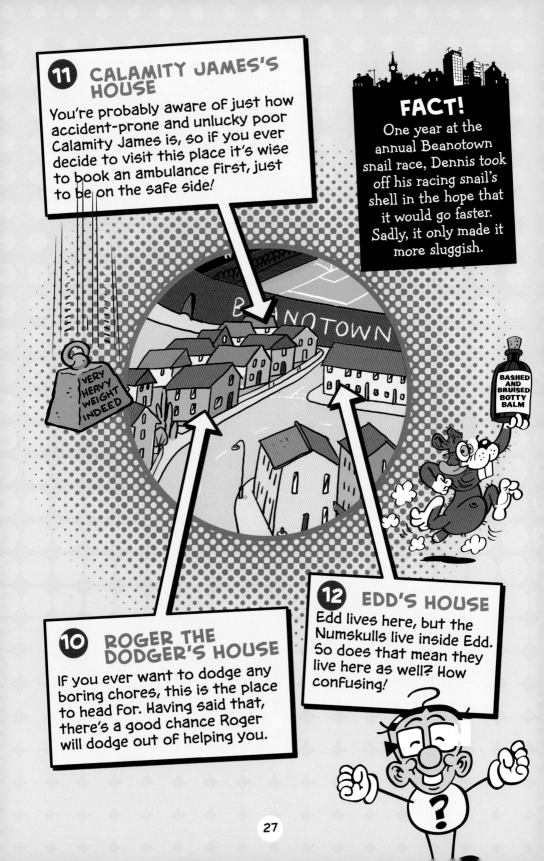

11 CALAMITY JAMES'S HOUSE

You're probably aware of just how accident-prone and unlucky poor Calamity James is, so if you ever decide to visit this place it's wise to book an ambulance first, just to be on the safe side!

FACT!

One year at the annual Beanotown snail race, Dennis took off his racing snail's shell in the hope that it would go faster. Sadly, it only made it more sluggish.

VERY HEAVY WEIGHT INDEED

BASHED AND BRUISED BOTTY BALM

10 ROGER THE DODGER'S HOUSE

If you ever want to dodge any boring chores, this is the place to head for. Having said that, there's a good chance Roger will dodge out of helping you.

12 EDD'S HOUSE

Edd lives here, but the Numskulls live inside Edd. So does that mean they live here as well? How confusing!

WALTER

NAME: Walter Brown, aka Walter the Softy, King of the Softies.

AGE: He can't wait to be 47 years old!

FAVOURITE BANK ACCOUNT: His Swiss Piggy Bank.

PETS: His luvvly wuvvly pet poodle, Foo Foo, and his lickle wickle Kitty Claudius.

HATES: Children who act their ages, and not like responsible adults. People who ask if they can use his parents' heated swimming pool.

LIKES: Snitching on kids who have fun. Getting expensive treats whilst making sure other kids don't get any.

ALL ABOUT WALTER

The undisputed high chieftain of all that is soft, Walter is Dennis's arch-nemesis. He likes nothing better than going to school (extra early) and doing his homework (twice). In fact, if Dennis hates it, you can be sure that Walter loves it. Walter is anti-fun, anti-kids and anti-aunties (probably, unless it's his rich aunt who gives him stuff).

My Favourite Things (by Walter)

As well as ruining people's fun and reminding everyone just how clever and grown-up I am, I also like other things, too! Here are some of my favourites:

★ Dressing Foo Foo up as a no-good peasant and playing a lovely game of 'I Run the Country'.

★ Chasing after rainbows to find a pot of gold (Daddy says you can never have enough gold).

★ Shaking my head and tutting when other children go past my house. When I'm in an especially good mood I also like to roll my eyes!

A Day in my Extraordinary Life

By Walter Brown Esq.

SATURDAY

6 a.m.   I wake early and listen to some complicated jazz music. Jazz is very clever and for grown-ups, but I'm very mature so I like it. Of course, I don't listen to any music that's loud. I wouldn't want to annoy my parents! Or hurt my ears – they're very sensitive, you know.

7 a.m.   I greet the milkman at the front door and remind him just how clever I am and how stupid he is. Hah hah!

9 a.m.   Breakfast. I like to eat my cornflakes out of a golden bowl. Then I help Mummy with the washing-up. We don't actually wash anything though. We just throw it all away. Because we are very rich.

10 a.m.   I go outside for a nice long walk. I'm not interested in the exercise, but it gives me a great opportunity to stop others from having fun. If I see anyone doing anything they shouldn't, I go and tell their parents!

1 p.m.   After many hours of being a killjoy, I get very hungry, so I trot home for a spot of lunch. Sandwiches, eaten off a golden plate. Again, I help Mummy with the dishes by throwing all the golden plates in the bin.

2 p.m.   Time for a nap, where I dream of being a spoilsport.

I am a big wally who smells.

Ha! I nicked Walter's stupid boring diary!
Dennis   30

A Guide To Teddykins

My teddy, Teddykins, is a very special bear. Here I explain all his lovely parts. (Note: don't ask to borrow him. He's mine and you can't have him. You're lucky I'm even showing him to you.)

Peepers – for looking down on other teddies with.

Arms – for pointing out things that other teddies are doing wrong.

Earholes – for listening to TV programmes about jazz and politics.

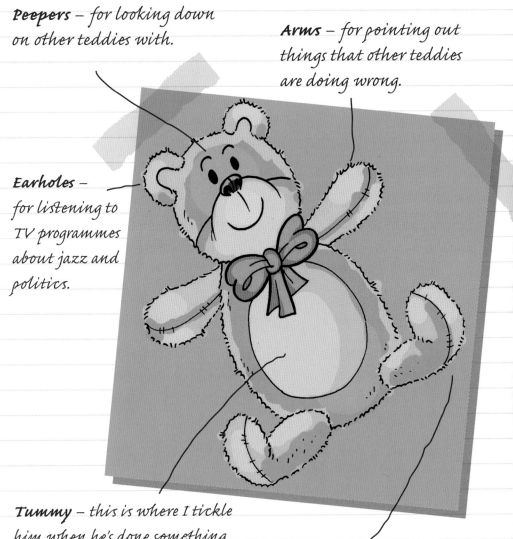

Tummy – this is where I tickle him when he's done something good (like scowl at someone).

Tootsies – these have no function.

MINNIE THE MINX

NAME: Minnie the Minx.

FAVOURITE TOY: A doll (you can rip the head off and use it as ammo for your catapult).

PETS: Chester the cat.

HATES: Boys who think that they're tougher than her (they aren't).

LIKES: Chips (the potato kind) and chops (the karate kind).

Minnie doesn't like snobs or Softies, which means she gets on really well with Dennis (unless he says he's tougher than her).

32

ALL ABOUT MINNIE

Minnie is tougher than any boy in Beanotown and prefers mischief to toy dolls and little tea sets. She hates the fact that the boys seem to get all the good toys (catapults, stink bombs, etc.) while everyone expects her to dress up like a princess just because she's a girl. By the way, be sure not to call her 'princess', because you'll probably get a thump.

JOKE BOX

BASH

MINNIE'S MAXIMUM MINXES

- Make breakfast time more fun (for you) by hiding some fake insects in the jam jar.

- Keep a scrapbook – by keeping a note of all the scraps you have with boys.

- Help boring people finish their jigsaws quicker, by hiding most of the pieces.

- The library is a really good place to go if you're bored. Find the heaviest book there, and drop it on someone's toe.

Minnie's Guide to Photobombing

Beanotown's magnificent Town Hall!

Sadly, 'photobombing' doesn't involve blowing up photographs with a bomb. All you have to do is either stand behind someone while they're having their picture taken, or get in the way of whatever it is they are trying to take a picture of. Here are some of my favourite pictures that I've ruined.

FACT!

Three out of ten people in Beanotown suffer from sniffly, runny noses. The rest actually quite enjoy it.

The amazing wildlife on Duck Island!

Historic Beanotown
Library!

my mum's birthday
party!

My dad catching the
biggest fish ever!

YOU MUST BE...
JOE KING!

What do you call
a pig that does
karate?

A pork chop!

MEET THE LOCALS

CALAMITY JAMES

VERY HEAVY WEIGHT INDEED

NAME: Calamity James, AKA The World's Unluckiest Boy.

FAVOURITE PLACE: The Accident and Emergency department at Beanotown Hospital. People there are so friendly. They're like a second family!

PETS: Alexander Lemming, plummeting expert and squelchologist.

HATES: The awful bad luck he always seems to have.

LIKES: Not hurting himself (which is rare).

MEGA STINK BOMB

FIVE THINGS UNLUCKIER THAN CALAMITY JAMES

1. Errrrrm . . .
2. Well, there's . . .
3. How about . . .
4. Maybe . . .
5. Look, *nothing* is unluckier than Calamity James!

ALL ABOUT CALAMITY JAMES

If some people seem to be born lucky, then Calamity James seems to have been born unlucky. He's a walking magnet for bad luck, and it's not just him that seems to attract all the unfortunate things in the world – it's anyone standing near him.

That's probably why his only friend is Alexander Lemming. Alexander loves plummeting from high things, so bad luck isn't really a problem for him.

Beanotown A&E Incident Report Log

Selected incidents involving Mr C. James, as recorded by Dr. Seth O'Scope

Incident #3482

Patient reports stepping in a bucket and falling down some stairs, out through the front door and on to the back of a truck transporting horse poop.

Treatment: Ointment for a sore head, and a very long shower.

Incident #3928

Patient says he was hit on the head while trying to turn a horseshoe the right way up. Says it wasn't his day. Again.

Treatment: More sore-head ointment.

Incident #3710

Patient claims to have tripped over what he describes as a 'Little Squelchy Thing'. I have never seen or heard of such a creature. Patient is clearly delirious.

Treatment: A stern talking-to about making things up.

Incident #4216

Patient claims to have been "twanged in the eye" while walking past the Knicker Elastic Factory, causing him to walk into a wall and bump his head.

Treatment: Yet more sore-head ointment, and a map suggesting some routes that avoid the Knicker Elastic Factory testing sheds (and walls).

Incident #6012

Patient claims to have become trapped while putting on a jumper at Beanotown Aquarium, which then caused him to fall into the shark tank.

Treatment: Scissors to cut him free of the jumper. Plus lots of bandages. And some sore-head ointment, just in case.

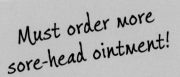

Must order more sore-head ointment!

YOU MUST BE...
JOE KING!

Doctor, my son has swallowed my pen! What should I do?

Use a pencil till I get there!

Squelchology

Part 2

A LITTLE HAIRY SQUELCHY THING

As the name suggests, the last place you'll find a Little Hairy Squelchy Thing is near a hairdresser's. Who knows why this shaggy little squidger refuses to get its long locks cut? Maybe it thinks short hair is for boring Squelchy Things. Actually, it could be that it's afraid of scissors.

A LITTLE BABY SQUELCHY THING

GOO! GOO! SQUELCH!

Hard to spot because it's so tiny and small. Scientists such as myself have yet to find out if the Little Baby Squelchy Thing will ever grow up. Maybe it'll simply stay a Little Baby Squelchy Thing for the rest of its little squelchy life. You might think it's not important – but it's not you who has to change all those squelchy nappies. POO-EE!

A LITTLE PIMPLY SQUELCHY THING

ZIT-FACED SQUELCH!

With more boils than a hundred kettles, the Little Pimply Squelchy Thing can be easily spotted by its zit-faced squelching. Worried that this little fella might not be squelchy enough? Fear not! When this particularly pimply thing pops its zits, it gets extra squidgy!

OCH! SEE YOU, SQUELCHY!

A LITTLE SCOTTISH SQUELCHY THING

Squelchier than a haggis packed full of extra-sticky raspberry jam, the Little Scottish Squelchy Thing comes from the wobbly Highlands, somewhere near the shores of Loch Squishy. When he isn't squishing his way across the hillsides, playing his beloved smooshpipes, the Little Scottish Squelchy Thing enjoys wobbling with friends, drinking squash and not being stepped on.

Out on the TOWN

14 COLD TRAFFORD

The home of Beanotown United, also known as the Theatre of Bad Dreams. This magnificent modern arena replaced United's former ground (The Beanotown United Thunderdome), and is known for its heaving match-day attendances of well over fifteen people (sometimes).

13 BALL BOY'S HOUSE

Home to Beanotown's biggest football fan! He lives so close to Cold Trafford that he can almost smell the goals (or at least he could if they ever scored any). When he's not outside playing football, you'll find him in here, eating his favourite meal: lukewarm pie garnished with half-time orange segments.

16 BILLY WHIZZ'S HOUSE

Home to the fastest boy on the planet! He'll answer the door before you ring the bell!

42

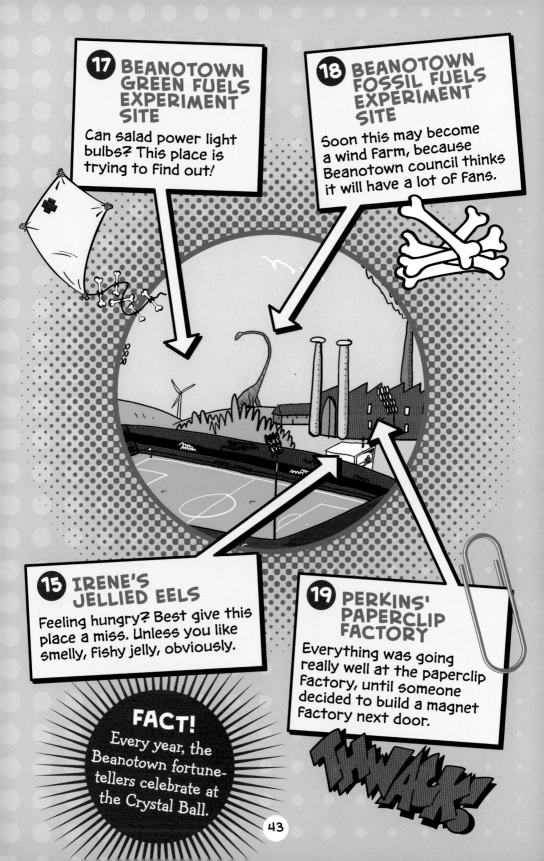

LES PRETEND

NAME: Lesley Presley Pretend.

PARENTS: Des Pretend and Mrs Pretend

PETS: His pretend crocodile is terrifying!

HATES: People with no imagination.

LIKES: Pretending to be anything he can think of.

LES NOT PRETEND

Sometimes Les's pretends are a bit rubbish and don't really work out as he imagined they would. Here are his biggest pretend-failures, so you don't make the same mistakes.

- Les once pretended to be a moth by eating his mum's jumpers (yuck!).

- Les once pretended to be a newspaper but got stuck in a letterbox (ouch!).

- Les once pretended to be an onion but was so good at it he made himself cry. He then had to pretend to be an ice cream to cheer himself up (yum!).

- Les once pretended to be a high court judge by wearing a wig made out of mini sausage rolls. He had to give up when he got chased by dogs (woof!).

DID YOU KNOW?

Les comes from a long line of pretenders. His great-grandfather, Harry 'Slippery' Pretend, once escaped a prison sentence by pretending to be innocent.

GASSY FIZZ

ALL ABOUT LES

Les is one of the most imaginative people in all of Beanotown, and likes to dress as up things he finds around the house. From a Martian to a mountain, you can be sure Les has dressed up as it, and has probably taken his Dad along for the adventure.

Les's Top Pretends

So, you want to be just like Les Pretend? The Great Pretender! The Pretendmaster General! El Pretendo Numero Uno! Les! Well, fix your peepers on this next bit. There are loads of things you can find around your house to help you turn into almost anything.

1 Use a bucket to pretend that either
a) you have a robot's head or
b) you are a talking bucket (with legs and arms and a body).

2 Strap a mattress to either side of your body to pretend you are a giant custard cream biscuit.

3 Pretend you are an archaeologist by digging up your parents' garden and finding the bones of the roast chicken you had for lunch last Sunday (remember to bury the bones the Sunday before for this one to work).

4 Repeatedly punch a garden hose to pretend you are a brave adventurer fighting a giant snake.

5 Stick a broom through your shirt sleeves and pretend to be a scarecrow (or someone who doesn't know how to use a broom properly).

1 x

36 x ha!

6 Pretend you are a giant by sitting on a bonsai tree and laughing.

MEET THE LOCALS

ROGER THE DODGER

NAME: Roger the Dodger, aka The Dodge, The Rodge, The Podge, Ro-Do (no one calls him any of those last things).

FAVOURITE COLOUR: Red. No wait, black. No, red. Red and black. Rack? Bled?

PARENTS: Yes thanks.

HATES: Homework, chores, homework about the history of chores and also chores that involve tidying up his homework.

LIKES: Books about dodges, long walks in the country (to get out of doing homework), the sound an angry dad makes ('harrrrmmpfffff').

DODGE FACTS

 Once Roger had a great idea for a dodge, but he didn't have a book to write it in, so he had to use loo roll instead (don't ever do the opposite of that, because they'll ask you to leave the library and never come back).

Roger is the same height as a stack of fifteen encyclopaedias. We know this because he once hid behind fifteen encyclopaedias to dodge a geography test.

In a particularly complicated dodge, Roger once used a dog dressed up as a unicorn to get out of helping his mum with the washing-up.

The elephant is the only animal that has four knees. This has absolutely nothing to do with Roger, but might still be handy to know!

The population of Beanotown was dramatically reduced in 1978, when an accident at the rotten egg factory meant that half the population had to go to Beanotown-on-Sea for a year to get some fresh air.

Roger writes all his dodges down in his Dodge Book. Its contents are top secret (or at least they will be until you turn the page!).

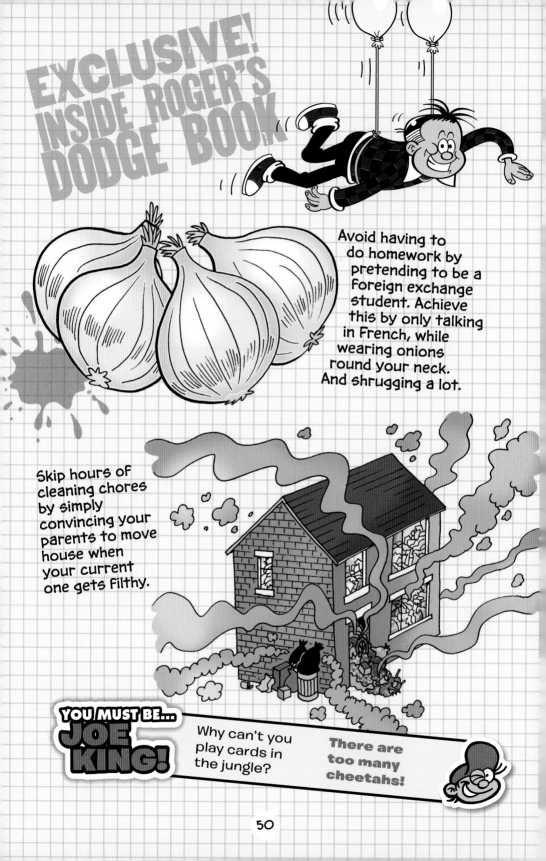

Avoid having to do homework by pretending to be a foreign exchange student. Achieve this by only talking in French, while wearing onions round your neck. And shrugging a lot.

Skip hours of cleaning chores by simply convincing your parents to move house when your current one gets filthy.

YOU MUST BE... JOE KING!

Why can't you play cards in the jungle?

There are too many cheetahs!

Dodge helping in the garden by throwing a bag of Flour into the air and running away. People will think you are a magician who has vanished in a puff of smoke.

FLOUR

Shirk housework by pretending World War III has started – no one will care about the dusting then!

Dig a tunnel through the Earth to get to Australia. They are eleven hours ahead of us, so technically you'll be in the future and all your chores will be in the past.

UK

AUSTRALIA

Squelchology
Part 3

A VERY SQUELCHY LITTLE SQUELCHY THING

The extra-squelchy nature of the Very Squelchy Little Squelchy Thing means it can smoosh under the gaps of doors. It can also be found inside postboxes, which it has quivered and squirmed its way into in order to find somewhere safe and dry from the rain. This explains why your letters are sometimes a bit squashy instead of nice and crispy.

SLITHER! SPLOO!

A LITTLE VIKING SQUELCHY THING

The Little Viking Squelchy Thing is known for two things: its skill with boats; and wearing a big pointy helmet. This little splodge may look fierce and scary, but you only have to worry if you live in an eleventh-century coastal village and you don't have squelch-proof doors. Pretty much everyone else is safe.

A VERY RUDE LITTLE SQUELCHY THING

SMELLY KNICKERS!

RAAAZZP!

Often found wiggling and sloshing around near raspberry bushes, the Very Rude Little Squelchy Thing is known for pushing into queues, making farty noises and shouting 'SMELLY KNICKERS!' at unsuspecting pensioners. This Squelchy's lack of manners is normally blamed on its parents, who gave it too much Fizzy Orange Guzzle Juice as a Squelchling.

WORM YOGHURT

A RATHER POSH LITTLE SQUELCHY THING

STUCK-UP SQUELCH!

More stuck up than a poster, the Rather Posh Little Squelchy Thing went to the best private school its parents could afford. Used to the finer things in life, it's no stranger to afternoons spent playing squashy polo, scoffing quails' eggs and squelching around wobblesome countryside estates. Sadly, it left an Eton mess behind and now has to hang around with all the other 'common' Little Squelchy Things, which causes it no end of distress. Poor little chap (not really).

Out on the TOWN

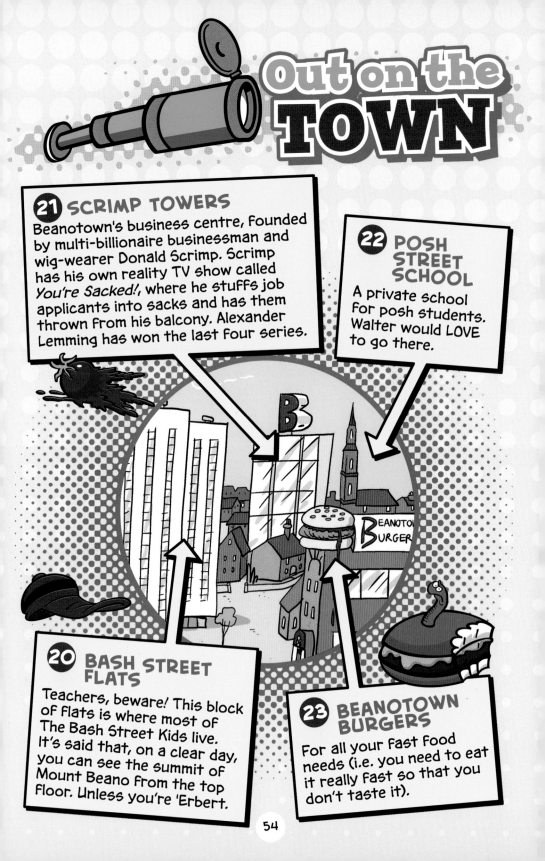

21 SCRIMP TOWERS

Beanotown's business centre, founded by multi-billionaire businessman and wig-wearer Donald Scrimp. Scrimp has his own reality TV show called *You're Sacked!*, where he stuffs job applicants into sacks and has them thrown from his balcony. Alexander Lemming has won the last four series.

22 POSH STREET SCHOOL

A private school for posh students. Walter would LOVE to go there.

20 BASH STREET FLATS

Teachers, beware! This block of flats is where most of The Bash Street Kids live. It's said that, on a clear day, you can see the summit of Mount Beano from the top floor. Unless you're 'Erbert.

23 BEANOTOWN BURGERS

For all your fast food needs (i.e. you need to eat it really fast so that you don't taste it).

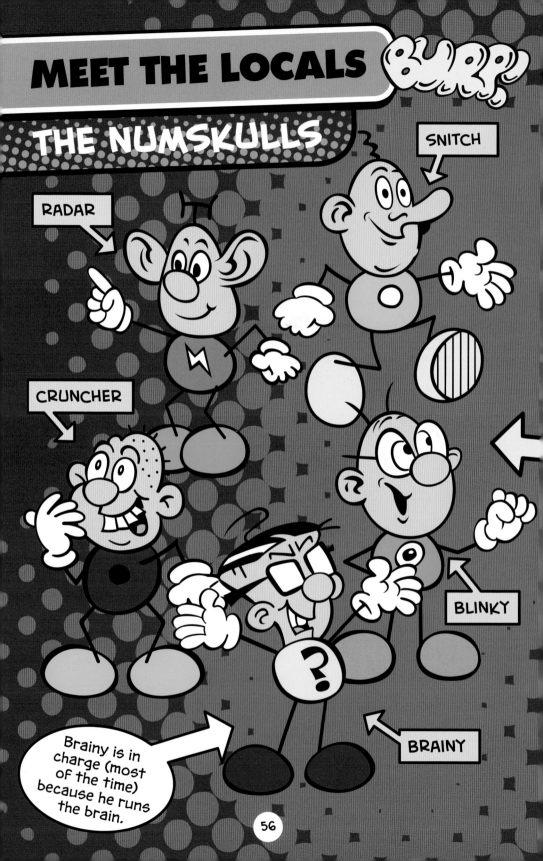

ALL ABOUT THE NUMSKULLS

AAA-CHOO!

The Numskulls live inside Edd's head and control everything he does: eating, thinking, sniffing, moving his arms around, making his knees twitch – you get the idea. When the Numskulls get along with each other, everything is fine in Edd's life – but sometimes the Numskulls bicker, which can get Edd into all kinds of scrapes.

Numskulls have even smaller Numskulls living inside them. And those Numskulls may even have Numskulls inside them too!

If you've ever had trouble waking up in the morning, that's because Blinky has overslept and forgotten to open your eyes.

ALL ABOUT EDD

Edd Case is your average boy. OK, so he's not too bright. In fact, he's a bit of a gormless nit – but that's not his fault, because he has Numskulls in his head, controlling him. We ALL have Numskulls inside our bodies . . . it's just that most people don't know about them.

Numskulls have to watch out for invasions from the rival Numskulls of other people/animals. If a dog's Numskulls were to get inside you, you'd end up barking mad (and burying bones).

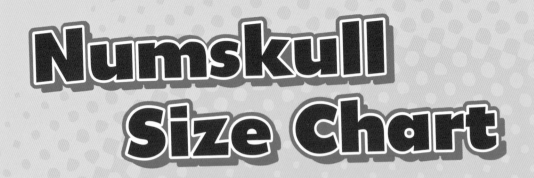

Numskull Size Chart

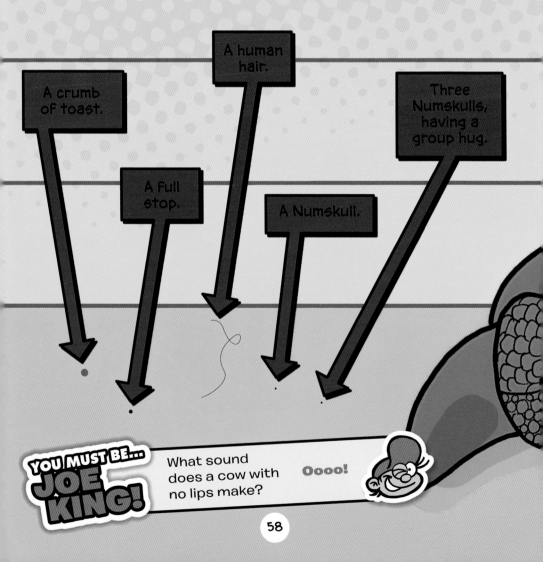

A crumb of toast.

A human hair.

Three Numskulls, having a group hug.

A full stop.

A Numskull.

YOU MUST BE...
JOE KING!

What sound does a cow with no lips make?

Oooo!

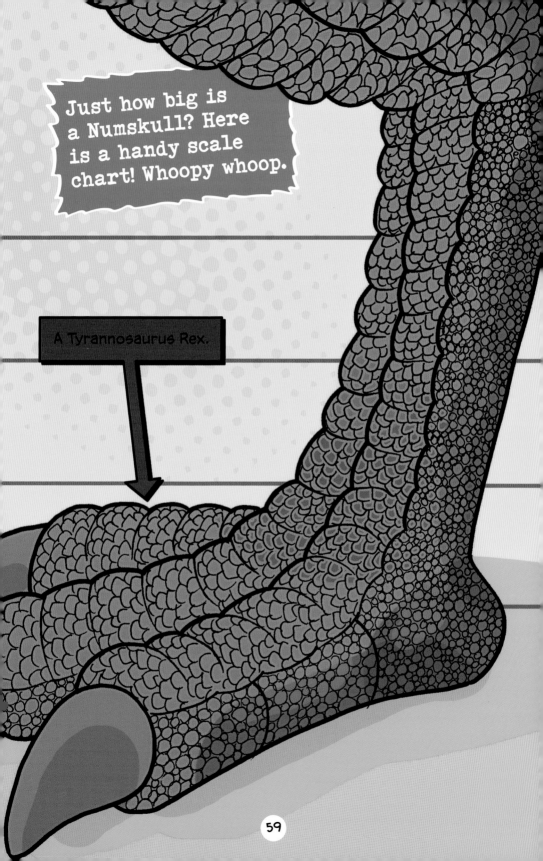

Numskull Map of the Human Body

Numskulls can be found all over your body, making sure it runs properly (most of the time). Here are some of the major departments that control things.

COLDSKULLS – GERM FIGHTING DEPT.

In charge of fighting off any nasty coughs, colds or fevers you might get.

TUMSKULLS – STOMACH DEPT.

The Tumskulls take care of the food that you eat, making sure that it gets all lovely and mushed up.

FACT!

A famous inventor from Beanotown was once convinced he could catch fog. He mist.

**DANCESKULLS –
HIP SWAYING DEPT.**

The special department is
needed whenever you dance.
If you are able to dance
well, that's because of your
Danceskulls. If you can't
dance well, that's because
you've taken them by surprise
(try letting them know in
advance next time).

**FOOTSKULLS –
WALKING DEPT.**

In charge of getting you
to walk, run and jump.
Occasionally one of them
might fall asleep and make
you fall over (being a
Numskull is tiring work).

**BUMSKULLS –
EMISSIONS
DEPT.**

The less said about
this department, the
better. Let's just
say they don't get
invited to very many
Numskull parties.

61

Numskulls in Edd's Head

BLINKY (EYE DEPT.)

Controls the eyes and is responsible for all things looky. Over the years, he's managed to get Edd to look in loads of different directions. Left, right . . . LOADS.

RADAR (EAR DEPT.)

Controls the ears and is responsible for hearing. Complains a lot about earwax (but, on the bright side, is never short of candles).

SNITCH (NOSE DEPT.)

Controls the nose and is responsible for sniffy/sneezy/snotty things.

CRUNCHER (MOUTH DEPT.)

Controls the mouth and taste buds. When Edd gets an urge to eat a pickled onion sandwich, or an entire choccy cake, or a gigantic sausage, it's because Cruncher is feeling peckish. When Edd gets an urge to lick a turnip, it's because Cruncher feels like having a bit of a laugh.

BRAINY (BRAIN DEPT.)

Controls the brain and thinky things. Brainy is the head of the NumSkulls. Which is a coincidence, because he also works inside a head. And he even has a head of his own. Which he is also the head of.

BILLY WHIZZ

NAME: Billy Whizz.

FAVOURITE SOUND: Sonic boom!

UNUSUAL FEATURE: That haircut. What DOES it look like?

HATES: Slowcoaches and pavement crawlers.

LIKES: Making supersonic jets look slow.

WORM YOGHURT

64

ALL ABOUT BILLY

Billy is the fastest boy in the world! Nobody on the planet is quicker than Billy, and he uses his faster-than-light speed to do everything.

His special whizz-speed means that he can cram more fun into his day than anyone else (actually, he could also cram in more rubbish stuff like homework if he wanted to, but who wants to do more homework?). It also means he can get into trouble extra quick, although he doesn't mean to - it's just that his legs are faster than his brain.

VROOM!

FACT!
The lift in the first skyscraper in Beanotown had to be taken out of service after it came down with something.

ZOOM!

FAST FACTS

★ Billy can run so fast he never gets wet when it rains.

★ Billy can't sit still for very long, which is why he never gets a proper haircut.

★ If a cheetah was to paint go-faster stripes on its sides and then fire itself from a cannon, Billy would still call it a slowcoach.

★ In the time it's taken you to read this sentence, Billy has read the entire book over fifty times! Why he didn't read fifty different books instead is something only he knows.

ZIP!

A rock
0 mph

Your granny carrying some heavy shopping
0.1 mph

An Olympic sprinter
27 mph

A cheetah
60 mph

A tomato fired by Dennis at a cheetah
68 mph

Dennis running away from an angry cheetah covered in bits of tomato
73 mph

A bolt of lightning hitting Dennis, who is running away from an angry cheetah covered in bits of tomato
203 mph

Billy Whizz
Whizz mph

Billy's Whizz-o-meter

JUST HOW FAST IS BILLY WHIZZ? THIS HIGHLY SCIENTIFIC COMPARISON OF SPEEDS WILL GIVE YOU A GOOD IDEA.

Squelchology

Part 4

OINK! HONK!

A LITTLE PIG-NOSED SQUELCHY THING

Earlier I mentioned that Squelchy Things evolve incredibly quickly, so it should come as no surprise that the Little Pig-nosed Squelchy Thing has taken on some porky characteristics. Some squelchologists believe this specimen displays the unpredictable natural beauty of evolution. Others think the little guy's just been eating too many bangers. Either way, the Little Pig-nosed Squelchy Thing is an oinksome treat and no mistake!

A LITTLE FLYING SQUELCHY THING

WARBLE! CHIRRUP!

Despite its confusing name, the Little Flying Squelchy Thing is not actually able to fly. This is because, as we all know, flight defies the laws of squelching. Still, those massive ears/wings sure do come in handy, especially for blowing out candles on its squishday cake (Happy Squishday!), or wafting away pongy smells caused by passing rear ends.

A BRAINY LITTLE EGGHEAD SQUELCHY THING

Are you having trouble working out a tricky bit of maths? Or perhaps you're doing a crossword and can't find the answer to four down? Then maybe the Brainy Little Egghead Squelchy Thing can help . . . as long as you don't mind all its wobbling, slithering and squirming, that is! Bring a towel to wipe all the squelch juice off, just in case.

A LITTLE FROGGY SQUELCHY THING

Bonjour! The Little Froggy Squelchy Thing is easy to spot – first with your nose (it smells of garlic) and then with your eyes (because of its big moustache and even bigger beret). Don't worry about language differences: all you need to know is that it's *très* squidgy, *très* wobbly and *très* squirmy, just like all the rest of the Squelchy Things.

GARLIC-SMELLING SQUELCH!

69

Out on the TOWN

28 BUNKERTON CASTLE

The home of Lord Marmaduke of Bunkerton, better known as Lord Snooty. He's posher than caviar-flavoured custard, but is loads of fun to hang out with (especially if he gives you a go in his private jet). Unfortunately, you can only visit if you're invited by the Lord himself (which isn't going to happen).

29 FORMER SITE OF BUNKERTON VILLAGE

This place spoiled the view from Bunkerton Castle's west wing, so Lord Snooty had it destroyed.

DOSH

DANGER!

31 PARKIE BOWLES'S HOUSE

The home of Parkie Bowles, Beanotown's greatest (and only) park keeper.

30 POSH TREES AND YETI

Bunkerton Estate's posh trees are home to one of Beanotown's most secretive creatures: the Sasquatch! Legend has it this ape-like creature was once commonly seen in the town, until one day it saw Plug's Family and ran for the safe shelter of the woods, never to return.

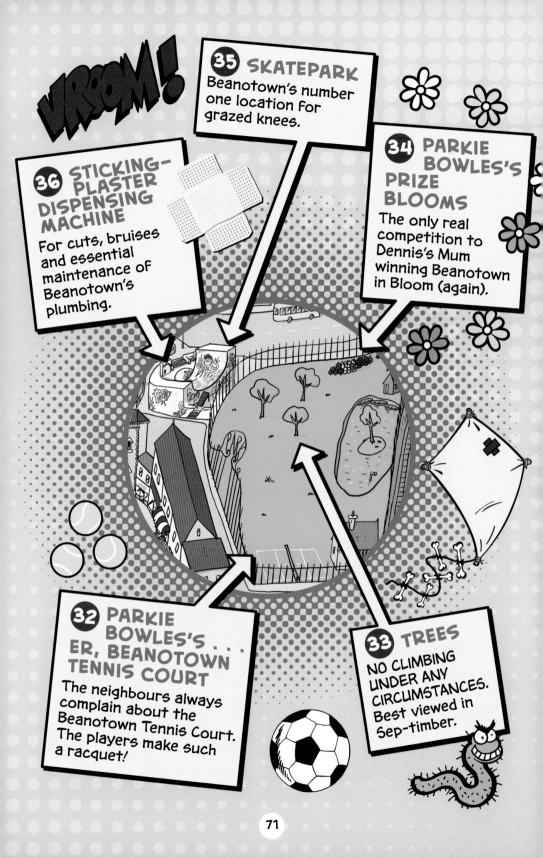

VROOM!

35 SKATEPARK
Beanotown's number one location for grazed knees.

36 STICKING-PLASTER DISPENSING MACHINE
For cuts, bruises and essential maintenance of Beanotown's plumbing.

34 PARKIE BOWLES'S PRIZE BLOOMS
The only real competition to Dennis's Mum winning Beanotown in Bloom (again).

32 PARKIE BOWLES'S . . . ER, BEANOTOWN TENNIS COURT
The neighbours always complain about the Beanotown Tennis Court. The players make such a racquet!

33 TREES
NO CLIMBING UNDER ANY CIRCUMSTANCES. Best viewed in Sep-timber.

Why not send your children to
Bash Street School?

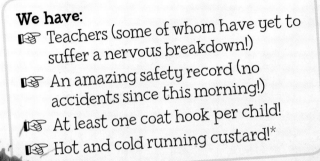

We have:
- ☞ Teachers (some of whom have yet to suffer a nervous breakdown!)
- ☞ An amazing safety record (no accidents since this morning!)
- ☞ At least one coat hook per child!
- ☞ Hot and cold running custard!*

*Sometimes. The rest of the time it's lukewarm and extra lumpy.

Meet the Bash Street Staff

Bash Street School is known for hiring the finest teachers. Admittedly, most of them left — but we found some others who say they're just as qualified! And who are we to judge?

HEADMASTER

Being a school headmaster suits my personality perfectly. I'm extremely calm, and even when I'm feeling a little stressed I never let it show.

TEACHER

I like teaching and I like my students. When I'm not teaching, I like lying down in a dark room with a cold towel over my eyes.

MRS CREECHER

I am a very dedicated teacher. Rules, regulations and times tables are my bread and butter. This is why I make horrible sandwiches.

OLIVE THE DINNER LADY

I am an incredible cook, making the most wonderful meals out of all kinds of ingredients. In my opinion, if food looks like it might still be alive, then that just means it's incredibly fresh.

JANITOR

There's always so much for me to do at Bash Street School, it's a wonder I find any time to sit in my office and play around with all the lost property and confiscated stuff. Busy, busy, busy — that's me!

WINSTON (JANITOR'S CAT)

Meow meow rrrrrrawww meow meow. Meow purrrr purrrrr purrrr meow. Raaaawwwrrr!
(Translation: I seem to do most of the work around here, while Janitor just sits in his office playing with catapults!)

Finding Your Way Around Bash Street School

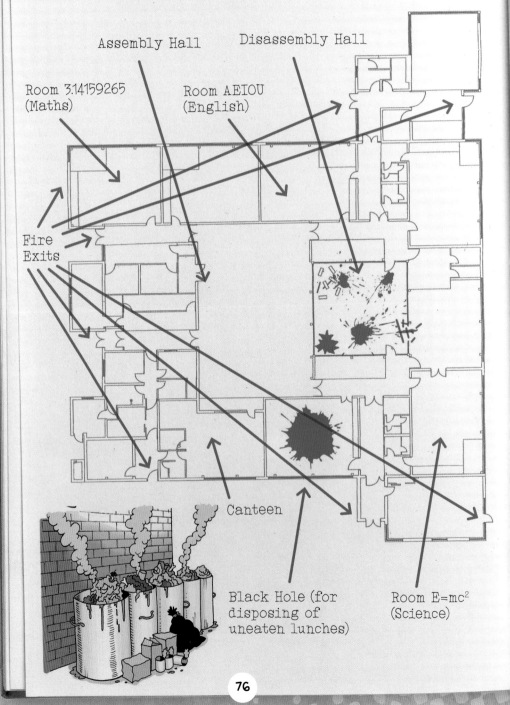

Assembly Hall

Disassembly Hall

Room 3.14159265 (Maths)

Room AEIOU (English)

Fire Exits

Canteen

Black Hole (for disposing of uneaten lunches)

Room E=mc² (Science)

The school inspector only had great things to say about Bash Street School!

'This is a ~~truly dreadful~~ school.'

'I've seen some ~~terrible~~ schools in my time, but Bash Street must be the single ~~worst~~ school I can remember.'

'The teachers are just ~~so bad it's~~ absolutely amazing. The students are ~~allowed to run amok in classes~~ – it's incredible.'

'They have a roof ~~which leaks.~~'

Olive's Canteen:
Behind the Beans Exclusive!

What's on the Menu at Olive's Canteen?
You can be sure of one thing –
it can be loosely referred to as 'food'.
Bon appetit!

Starters
Soup of the day (what day it was, we're not sure –
possibly a Thursday in 1992)

Mains
Roasted chunks of something
served with a hot grey sauce

Steamed chunks of something
served with a cold grey sauce

No chunks of anything
served with a grey dressing

Pudding
Steamed mess with extra-lumpy custard.
We-hope-it's-fruit salad

All meals are followed by
complimentary sore-tummy tablets

SCHOOL REPORT

BASH STREET SCHOOL

Name: Danny

Class: 2B

Teacher: Teacher

General Comments:

Danny shows excellent leadership skills and seems to have the respect of his fellow classmates. In fact, they'll do pretty much anything he says. This is not a good thing.

Science: B+

This term Danny has been demonstrating the science behind water pistols. He thoughtfully explained it to the rest of the class by squirting them in their faces. He then made sure they understood the science by squirting them again. He does this every day. Such commitment.

Pirate Studies: A+

Danny excels at this subject, even dressing the part!

SCHOOL REPORT

BASH STREET SCHOOL

Name: Smiffy

Class: 2B

Teacher: Teacher

General Comments:

Smiffy is not the brightest spark in the class. In fact, Smiffy is dimmer than a power cut in a coal mine at midnight. But he has a good heart — just don't ask him where his heart is, because he'll point at his foot.

Maths: D-

Smiffy thinks a times table is a desk with a clock on it.

Daydream Studies: A+

Smiffy shows great promise at staring into space for hours on end and not listening to anything anyone says. He'll make a great politician some day!

SCHOOL REPORT

Name: Fatty

Class: 2B

Teacher: Teacher

General Comments:
If Fatty showed as much enthusiasm for learning as he does for scoffing cakes and pies, he would make an excellent student. And the world would have a lot more cakes and pies.

Geography: C-
Disappointing. Fatty thought the classroom globe was a giant bonbon and spent most of this term licking it. Now almost all of Asia has disappeared from the map.

Home Economics: A-
Fatty seems to really engage with cookery lessons. When I taught the class about pie-making he couldn't wait for the finished results! So he started eating the oven.

SCHOOL REPORT

Name: Wilfrid

Class: 2B

Teacher: Teacher

BASH STREET SCHOOL

General Comments:

A very quiet boy, which comes as a welcome relief in Class 2B. I wish more students were like Wilfrid, then I wouldn't have so many headaches.

Maths: UNGRADED

Sorry, I don't remember this student at all. Was he the one sitting next to the big green tortoise?

Drama: A+

Excellent mime skills. He never breaks character to speak. This term he spent the entire time pretending to be a tree.

INVISIBLE INK

SCHOOL REPORT

Name: Spotty

Class: 2B

Teacher: Teacher

General Comments:
Quite a disruptive boy, always mouthing off and interrupting teachers. Nice tie, though.

Physical Education: D–
Gets easily upset during football matches if anyone calls him short. Good at tackling, though.

Maths: A+
A truly excellent student. Is easily able to count up to 976 using his face as a sort of bumpy calculator.

SCHOOL REPORT

Name: 'Erbert

Class: 2B

BASH STREET SCHOOL

Teacher: Teacher

General Comments:
Usually a very well-behaved boy, although I've noticed that he seems to be concentrating very hard all the time. Is it possible that he may have a very, very minor problem with his eyesight?

Art: E+
E+ Not a great student. This is supposed to be a picture of a bowl of fruit.

Science: B-
Gave the class a great demonstration of the power of solar energy when he left his glasses on his desk and the sun's rays shone through them, setting the entire school on fire.

SCHOOL REPORT

Name: Sidney

Class: 2B

Teacher: Teacher

General Comments:
Sidney is gifted with a great sense of humour.
Perhaps one day he'll become a comedian. Or use
his hair to sweep out chimneys.

Geography: C–
Quite a disruptive influence in the classroom.
In one lesson he turned all the maps upside
down and convinced me that I was using
Australian maps.

Physical Education: B+
Excellent team player. Unfortunately the team he
played for was made up of his pets — twelve mice,
an elephant and two crocodiles.
The clean-up operation afterwards
took several weeks.

SCHOOL REPORT

Name: Toots

BASH STREET SCHOOL

Class: 2B

Teacher: Teacher

General Comments:
Shows good leadership skills, although sometimes she insists on everyone calling her 'Your Majesty' and threatens to send people to the dungeons if she doesn't like them.

Business Studies: D+
Spent the whole of last term telling everyone in the class that they were 'fired!'. Despite what she may have heard, this is not a good way to get ahead in the business world.

Music: A-
She absolutely adores music, although if she would take her headphones off once in a while she might hear me talking about music, rather than just listening to it.

SCHOOL REPORT

Name: Plug

Class: 2B

Teacher: Teacher

General Comments:
A really wonderful addition to Class 2B, especially when he turns round and faces the back of the classroom.

English: A+
Please, I'll give you whatever grade you want! Just don't make me look at your ugly mug ever again . . .

History: A+
The horror! The horror! So many nightmares.

Visit the Beefo Burger Van™ Today!

Feeling hungry? Avoiding school dinners again? Would you like a burger that might be made of meat? Then you're in luck! The Beefo Burger Van™ is here to serve you, no questions asked!*

To find your local Beefo Burger Van™, just follow your nose. We smell of burnt meat and oil, so we're easy to find!

*You don't ask any questions, OK?

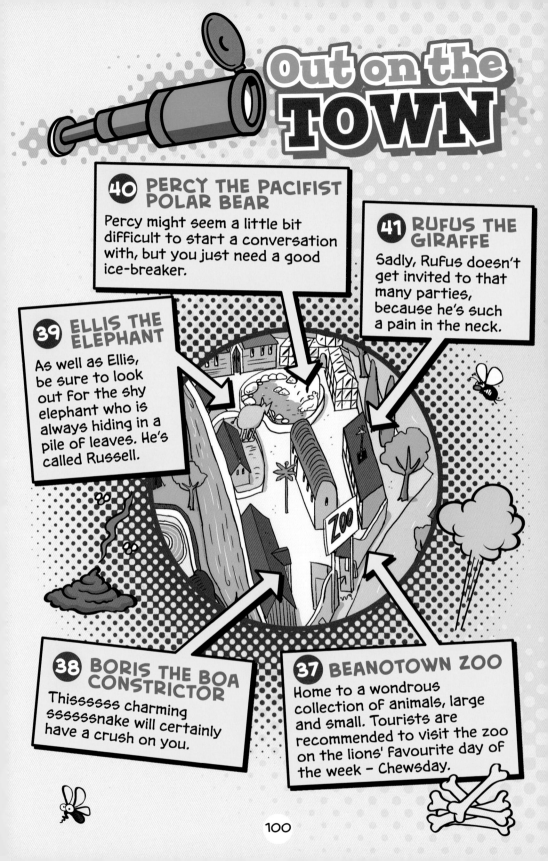

Out on the TOWN

40 PERCY THE PACIFIST POLAR BEAR
Percy might seem a little bit difficult to start a conversation with, but you just need a good ice-breaker.

41 RUFUS THE GIRAFFE
Sadly, Rufus doesn't get invited to that many parties, because he's such a pain in the neck.

39 ELLIS THE ELEPHANT
As well as Ellis, be sure to look out for the shy elephant who is always hiding in a pile of leaves. He's called Russell.

38 BORIS THE BOA CONSTRICTOR
Thissssss charming sssssssnake will certainly have a crush on you.

37 BEANOTOWN ZOO
Home to a wondrous collection of animals, large and small. Tourists are recommended to visit the zoo on the lions' favourite day of the week – Chewsday.

45 BEANOTOWN CINEMA

What could be showing at Beanotown Cinema this week? Whatever it is, it's probably reel-y good.

FROM A FRIEND

44 WIDL

The best supermarket in town for the cost-conscious shopper. This week they have cheap venison, which isn't too deer. Oh, and they're also selling half-price couches, for customers with a suite tooth.

GASSY FIZZ

EXTRA LARDY CRISPS

42 ERIC'S HOUSE

Number 29 Acacia Road is the home of Eric Wimp, a boy who leads an exciting double life. That's right – as well as being a schoolboy, he's also in the scouts! Hmm, actually there might be something else too . . .

43 NUMBER 13 FRIGHTVILLE AVENUE

The spookiest, ghouliest house in Beanotown. It doesn't have a 'living' room.

Teacher's Secret Diary

Saturday

Hooray! Saturday! The first time in a week that I'm not surrounded by rude people shoving me about. I think I'll go to the shops, which are going to be . . . er . . . full of rude people shoving me about.

Sunday

Today I had a lovely Sunday lunch with Mrs Teacher. Then I spent the entire afternoon trying not to think about going back to school tomorrow. What a perfect end to a weekend.

FACT!
The saddest person who ever lived in Beanotown was called Lee, and nobody ever talked to him. He was lone-lee.

Monday

One of my students brought me an apple.
How thoughtful! I have the
best students in the world.
Unfortunately, Fatty ate it
five minutes later.

Tuesday

Another challenging day of teaching. Well, that's what
I got into this profession for – to be challenged! I just
didn't realize it would be so
tiring. I asked young Smiffy
why he thought the weather
in Britain was so wet, and he
replied, 'Because the Queen
has had a long reign.'

Wednesday

Headmaster tried to have a 'chat' with me about Class 2B today – he doesn't seem to like them very much. I said that's because he doesn't really know them. Then he got a bit angry thinking about them, so I used a cup of Olive's 'tea' to burn a hole in the wall and make my escape.

Thursday

Woke up this morning thinking it was Friday. It's not. Still, those pupils won't teach themselves! In class today Sidney lost one of his pet mice. It later turned up inside my trousers, which I'm confident was a complete coincidence.

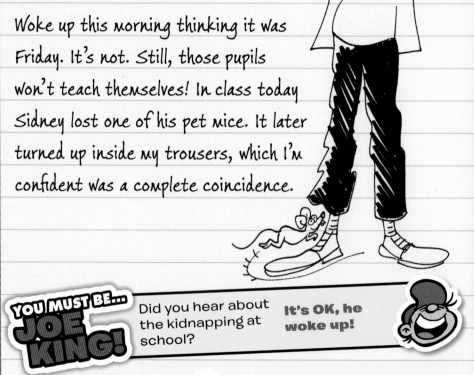

YOU MUST BE... JOE KING!

Did you hear about the kidnapping at school?

It's OK, he woke up!

Friday

It's. Almost. The. Weekend. I. Can't. Wait. I. Also.
Can't. Write. Sentences. Any. More. So. Very. Tired.
Is. It. Saturday. Yet?

Fatty's Fave Snacks

Hello, readers! In between meals I like to enjoy the odd snack or two to keep my strength up. Here are some of my favourites!

Fatty's Food Facts Ketchup can also be used as a refreshing drink.

The Leaning Tower Of Pasta

A plate of pasta so tall it looks like it's about to topple over. The trick is to eat it as quickly as possible.

Hamburgers

I don't know why they call them hamburgers when they are made of beef. I like proper hamburgers — twenty slices of ham, then a burger, topped off with another twenty slices of ham. Food should be called what it is. Don't get me started on fish fingers.

Fatty's Food Facts Moving my jaw so much to eat food burns a lot of calories. This is why I have such a trim, muscular physique!

Birthday cake

With billions of people on the planet, it's always someone's birthday — so why not have a big slice of cake to celebrate? Then have another slice thirty seconds later, because it's someone else's birthday by then.

These clever diagrams illustrate statistically what I like to eat. I'm getting hungry just looking at them!

Fatty's Food Facts
Apples are 25 per cent air. That's why chocolate is better value for money.

A burger

Bit of a burger with some ketchup on it

Pizza

Bit of pizza that I have just scoffed

All chips are good chips!

Length of chips

chips

Fatty's Food Facts
Turn salad into something tasty by emptying a bucket of gravy over it.

Smiffy's Photo Album

Smiffy loves to take photos. He's not very good at it, but that doesn't stop him from trying. Smiffy can be very trying sometimes. Here are some of his best snaps.

My pet pebble, Kevin!

SELFIE.

Everyone in class 2B!

Is this a King Kong?

on holiday at
Beanotown-on-sea!

What I had for lunch today.

YOU MUST BE...
JOE KING!

What do you call a cow that gives no milk?

An udder failure!

Bash Street School Noticeboard

Free Pea-shooter Ammunition

Help yourself! Just take this bit of paper, screw it up into a little ball and fire at will!

Cuthbert Cringeworthy's After-school School

Not getting enough school in your school day? Then join Cuthbert and other like-minded pupils for extra school. The teachers will love us for it!

Cringeworthy's After-school School – It's exactly like school, but even longer!

Cuthbert Cringeworthy's After-after-school-school School

Not getting enough school at Cuthbert Cringeworthy's After-school School? Then join Cuthbert and other like-minded pupils for even more school. The teachers are getting a bit tired of it, but they probably still love us, right?

Cringeworthy's After-after-school-school School – it's exactly like After-school School, but even longer!

MISSING PET

Answers to the name of 'Cuddles'. Has a wonderful smile and is a snappy dresser. Missing since last week – if you find him (or if he finds you), please contact Sidney IMMEDIATELY.

The Bash Street Burp

SPECIAL EDITION!

Inside this edition of The Bash Street Burp:

☆ An exclusive interview with Teacher!

☆ Toots's Top Ten Tunes!

☆ What's on at Bash Street
this week?

☆ Puzzles!

EXCLUSIVE INTERVIEW!

This week we meet the one and only Teacher! Plug and 'Erbert caught up with him to ask him some very important questions.

Bash Street Burp: Hi, Teacher! How are you today?

Teacher: . . .

BSB: Hellooooooooo, Teacher! We know you're in there.

Teacher: I'm, er, just having a quick break. I might have a bit of a headache.

BSB: In the stationery cupboard?

Teacher: Yes. I also needed a pencil.

BSB: Will you come out and talk to us?

Teacher: I'd love to! But I've lost the key to the door, so I'm locked in here.

BSB: But the door doesn't have a lock.

Teacher: Oh yes, right. Well, what's happened is that a chair has fallen over against the door, and now I can't open it.

BSB: So you can't come out?

Teacher: Sadly, no. I'll just have to stay here and rest for a bit. Yes, rest. Quietly.

BSB: Shall we get Janitor to help you?

Teacher: No, no, it's fine. I'll work it out. You go and torment . . . I mean play with . . . someone else.

BSB: OK then, bye! We'll just leave this stink bomb here for you so you have something to do.

YOU MUST BE... JOE KING!

What do you get if you walk under a cow?

A pat on the head!

Toots's Top Ten Tunes!

This week's top ten best bands, as rated by our resident music expert, Toots Pye.

1. Lipp Sync, 'Someone Else Is Singing This'
2. The Beanotown Bakers, 'Knead-To-Know Basis'
3. The Calendars, 'Our Days Are Numbered'
4. The Chickens, 'Dancing Chick-to-Chick' (Poultry In Motion remix)
5. Craig Velcro, 'I'm Just A Rip-off'
6. Dead Batteries, 'We're Free Of Charge'
7. Mickey & The Cannibals, 'We Like To Meat People'
8. The Boiled Eggs, 'So Hard To Beat'
9. The Fogs, 'You'll Be Mist'
10. The Coffee Shop Crew, 'The Daily Grind'

Teacher's Top Five Places to Hide from Students

1. Under his desk
2. Under Headmaster's desk
3. Under Mrs Creecher's desk
4. Under Janitor's desk
5. Under Winston's kitty-litter tray

News & Events

What's on at Bash Street this week

Monday: The Great Bash Street Bake-off

Come and help raise money for local charities with a cake sale! Lots of cakes and biscuits on offer. Get here early! Or Fatty will have eaten the lot.

Thursday: Weekly 'Guess What We Ate For Lunch?' Competition

Pupils and staff are once again encouraged to guess what we all had for lunch today. The winner will receive a lunch voucher to be spent anywhere that isn't Olive's canteen! Last week's winner was Wilfrid, who correctly guessed that we had 'something disgusting' for lunch. Well done, Wilfrid! Your voucher is in the post!

Friday: Commemorative Plaque Unveiling with Smiffy

Join Smiffy for a very special ceremony, when he unveils a memorial plaque to one of Bash Street's most famous ex-pupils, Mr Fire Exit. (It's just a fire exit sign, but don't tell Smiffy. He's made a little pair of curtains for the plaque and everything.)

FIRE Exit

Bash Street Brainbashers
Bash your brain with these fiendish puzzles!

What's on Danny's Mind?
Fill in the missing letters to reveal what Danny is thinking about.

P _ R _ T _ S

Count Spotty's Spots
How many spots is Spotty covered with?

[ ] spots

Fatty's Word Search
What is Fatty thinking about?

```
F O O D F O O D F D
O F O O D O O F O O
O O F O O D O O O O
D O O F F O F D D F
O D O O D O O F O O
O F D O O F O O D O
F O O D D F D D O D
O O D O O F O O O O
O F O O D D O O F O
D F D D O O F F D F
```

ANSWERS

What's on Danny's Mind?
PIRATES. Not parrots!

Count Spotty's Spots
You can see 30 spots (but there are a LOT more).

Fatty's Word Search

MEET THE LOCALS

THE BASH STREET PUPS

TUBBY

Will eat anything. Once got stuck in a hole in a fence while trying to get to some sausages that were lurking on the other side. It wasn't a problem though, as he ate the fence.

PEEPS

The Princess of Pups. She bosses all the other dogs about, especially if Bones is away.

'ENRY

Thankfully 'Enry has a great sense of smell, because he can't see very well.

SNIFFY

Sniffy gets confused about where he's hidden his bones (and what bones are in the first place). Once tried to bury a small car by mistake (to be fair, it did smell of ham).

WIGGY
Peeps's brother. Has the strongest fur for miles around. Once got a part-time job with some builders, who used him as sandpaper to get paint off a fence.

PUG
Winner of the Beanotown Woofts Dog Show (in the category of 'ugliest dog ever').

BLOTTY
Is Blotty covered in spots or are they just fleas? (Big hint: they're definitely spots.)

BONES
The leader of the pack. This is why he gets the first pick of meaty loot nicked from the butcher's shop.

MANFRID
Owner of the biggest dog collar in all of Beanotown. It's perfect for hiding his chops in.

Out on the TOWN

46 WHERE THE SQUELCHY THINGS ARE

The Squelchy Things live underground, but as they're the fastest-growing life form on the planet it's only a matter of time before they run out of underground and spill out to the overground. Then we're for it.

48 THE LAKE MESS MONSTER

Legend has it that this lake is inhabited by a fearsome monster. People would probably see it more, but it likes to play Koi and is very shellfish (that doesn't even make sense – Ed).

47 LAKE MESS

Home to a wide variety of fish, as well as a growing number of shopping trolleys.

49 BEANOTOWN CAMPSITE

Set up your tent and gather round the campfire to sing songs like 'Why Are We Here Again?' and 'I'm Freezing and Miss My Bed'.

53 THE THREE BEARS' CAVE

Boasting great views of Greedy Gulch, the Three Bears' Cave is also within pie-sniffin' distance of Hank's windowsill.

Every year, Beanotown hosts a party. A local boxer always brings the punch.

CACTUSVILLE

52 HANK'S 24-HOUR VARMINT HUNTING SUPPLIES CONVENIENCE STORE

Hank's store never closes, and sells a variety of blunderbusses, blunderbuss ammunition and blunderbuss accessories (including T-shirts, mugs and novelty five-foot-long pencils).

50 TRADITIONAL SMELLYFEET DWELLING

Also known as a tipi.

51 TRADITIONAL SMELLYFEET TOILET

Also known as a peepee.

Squelchology

Part 5

A VERY SHY LITTLE SQUELCHY THING

BLUSH!

BLAZE!

One of the hardest Squelchy Things to spot, as it's almost always in hiding and doesn't like to be seen. It does like to be heard, though, so if you've ever heard any sloshy, squashy or slithery sounds and you can't see where they're coming from, you know who is responsible.

A MICROSCOPIC LITTLE SQUELCHY THING

Don't expect to see the teeny tiny weeny Microscopic Little Squelchy Thing unless you walk around with microscopes strapped to your eyes, which is something I would not advise as a) you'll look really weird and b) you'll end up walking into things and will hurt yourself. Although small, the Microscopic Little Squelchy Thing does hold the world record for having the loudest squelch in proportion to its body size.

AN EVIL LITTLE VAMPIRE SQUELCHY THING

More sucky than a warehouse full of vacuum cleaners, the Evil Little Vampire Squelchy Thing can be found slurping and burping its way around Beanotown after midnight. As you might have guessed, the Evil Little Vampire Squelchy Thing craves blood – but, if you find yourself being chased by one, you can easily distract it with a big squirt of ketchup. It may be evil and squelchy, but it's not too smart. Besides, it quite likes ketchup, too, so everyone's happy.

SLURP! BURP!

TYPE O

A SKINNYMALINKY LITTLE SQUELCHY THING

SCRAWNY SQUELCH!

The scrawniest squelcher I have yet to encounter, the Skinnymalinky Little Squelchy Thing is tall and thin like a skyscraper. Thankfully though, skyscrapers don't quiver and slosh and jiggle about as much as this Squelchy Thing, otherwise nobody who works in them would ever get anything done (unless slipping around on squelch-juice counts as doing something).

YOU MUST BE... JOE KING!

What flies and wobbles at the same time?

A jellycopter!

MEET THE LOCALS

BALL BOY

NAME: Ball Boy.

PETS: His pet ball, Goaly McKicky.

HATES: Fouls.

LIKES: Goals!

ALL ABOUT BALL BOY

GOOOOOOAAAAAALLLLLLLLL!!!!!!!!!
Ball Boy doesn't just like football; he LOVES football. There's not a minute of the day that goes by when he isn't thinking about the beautiful game. Even when he's asleep he dreams about it. Once, he kicked his pillow through the window while dreaming about the World Cup. His only 'goal' in life is to play and watch and talk about football as much as he can.

BALL BOY'S TROPHY CABINET

WINNER: BALL BOY
For talking about football the most.

WINNER: BALL BOY
For thinking about football the most.

WINNER: BALL BOY
For dreaming about football the most.

WINNER: BALL BOY
For scoring a goal wearing a silly hat.

YOU MUST BE...
JOE KING!

Why did Cinderella get kicked out of the football team?

Because she kept running away from the ball!

Ball Boy's Guide to the
Beautiful Game

Here are some amazing football facts you probably didn't Know!

FOOTFACT!
The first red card used by a referee was actually a menu for a pizza restaurant.

Pizza

ALL THE TOPPINGS ALL THE SIZES

FRESHLY MADE

Ball Boy's Pick: Teams You Should Support (Because They Are Good)

Mudchester United
Shellsea F.C.
Notvery Athletic F.C.
Everytown F.C.
Buckingham Palace F.C.

FOOTFACT!
Horses are not allowed to play professional football because they have too many legs and it gives them an unfair advantage.

Why was the football pitch wet?

Because the players kept dribbling on it!

FOOTFACT!

Footballs got their name because they are ball-shaped and you kick them with your foot. In the early days, they were almost called 'toe-rounds', but everyone realized how silly that sounded. Phew!

FOOTFACT!

The first player to do a special celebration dance after scoring a goal wasn't actually dancing – he thought he had a spider on his back and was trying to get rid of it.

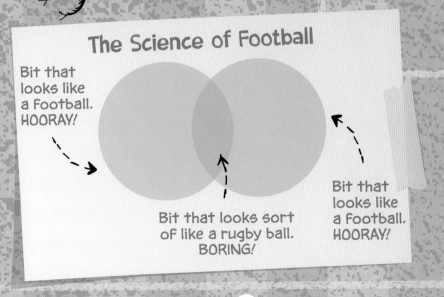

The Science of Football

Bit that looks like a Football. HOORAY!

Bit that looks sort of like a rugby ball. BORING!

Bit that looks like a Football. HOORAY!

Ball Boy Explains the Offside Rule in a Very Simple Way

Many people who watch football complain about not understanding the offside rule. Many more claim to understand it, but they are WRONG. Let me explain to you how the offside rule works, with this simple diagram.

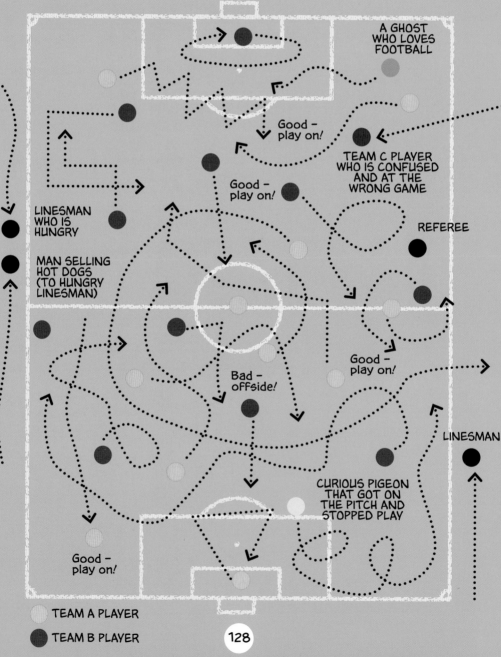

A GHOST WHO LOVES FOOTBALL

Good – play on!

TEAM C PLAYER WHO IS CONFUSED AND AT THE WRONG GAME

Good – play on!

REFEREE

LINESMAN WHO IS HUNGRY

MAN SELLING HOT DOGS (TO HUNGRY LINESMAN)

Good – play on!

Bad – offside!

LINESMAN

CURIOUS PIGEON THAT GOT ON THE PITCH AND STOPPED PLAY

Good – play on!

○ TEAM A PLAYER

● TEAM B PLAYER

MEET THE LOCALS

LORD SNOOTY

NAME: Lord Marmaduke of Bunkerton, aka Lord Snooty, aka His Poshness.

FAVOURITE COLOUR: Gold.

PETS: Does his faithful butler, Parkinson, count as a pet?

HATES: Poor people (by 'poor people', he means anyone who doesn't live in a castle).

LIKES: Money!

DOSH DOSH

ALL ABOUT LORD SNOOTY

Lord Snooty looks down on everyone – not just because he's posh but because the castle he lives in has a really high turret with a great view looking down over everyone. The turret does have a lot of steps up to it, though, so he has to get a piggyback from his butler, Parkinson. When not looking down on everyone, Lord Snooty enjoys eating from a silver spoon (he has thousands) and rolling around in gold coins (his expensive doctor told him it's good for his bad back).

PARKINSON'S PREMIER PUT-DOWNS

One of my great pleasures in life is to murmur sarcastic put-downs behind Lord Snooty's back. Here are some of my favourites for taking his Lordship down a peg or two (without him knowing, obviously).

- When Lord Snooty is playing golf and he tells me to bring him his tee, I ask if he would like it with milk and sugar.

- When Lord Snooty asks for a cucumber sandwich, I slice a cucumber in two and put a slice of bread between the two halves. He needs to be more specific!

- In the evenings, when Lord Snooty orders me to 'draw him a bath', I hand him a picture of the bath I've just sketched.

- When I bring Lord Snooty his dinner, sometimes I just bring him a plate of vegetables. When he asks where the meat is, I say it was a 'mis-steak'.

BEANOTOWN CRiBS
with Lord Snooty

I don't usually let the likes of you into Bunkerton Castle. It's normally just really posh and rich people that I like to invite over. But on this occasion I'll make an exception (just to make you jealous, hah hah!). Here are some of the incredible things you would see if I let you past the front door . . .

Bejewelled big-screen TV

What's better than the world's largest television? The world's largest television encrusted with jewels and diamonds, that's what! Every square centimetre of this 560-inch beast is covered in expensive jewels, rubies and diamonds. Even the screen, which means I can't actually watch anything on it. But that's not the point – the point is that I own it.

Jacuzzi bath with hot and cold running champagne

Obviously I could never take a bath in tap water. Do you know what's in that stuff? No, neither do I, and I don't want to find out. After a long day of walking around my massive house I can feel a tad grubby, so I like to ease myself into a giant Jacuzzi filled with the finest champers. The Jacuzzi makes the bubbles extra bubbly, which is what I deserve. I am a lord, after all.

Huge mysterious room

I'm not saying my house is so big that I don't even know what's in all the rooms, but . . . well, OK, that's exactly what I'm saying. My house is so big that I don't even know what's in all the rooms! Like this one, for example. All I know is that it seems massive and is probably full of gold . . . stuff.

Antique vase collection

This room is where I keep my collection of priceless antique vases. I have extra high-level security here as I don't want anyone to break in and knock all the vases over (I'd have to buy lots more, and shopping is just so tiresome). Actually, I probably shouldn't have lined them all up like dominos . . .

Servants' quarters

I've almost run out of room for storing all my top hats, so I might have to kick the servants out so I can use their rooms.

Out on the TOWN

57 FROSTY JIM
Every day at around lunchtime you can find Jim tucking into an iceberger.

56 MOUNT BEANO
Beanotown's highest peak is a world-renowned snowball-throwing resort tragically ignored by the organizers of the Winter Olympics, who continue to insist that chucking snowballs at teachers is not a proper winter sport.

CROSSPATCH NUTTY TOWN

BEANOTOWN

55 THE WORLD-FAMOUS BEANOTOWN SIGN
People come from far and wide to see the world-famous Beanotown sign. OK, one person came once to see the sign. Clearly they forgot to tell all their friends about it.

54 DAVE THE GOAT
Poor old Dave. He doesn't even know how he goat here.

58 BEANOTOWN OBSERVATORY

The scientists at the Beanotown Observatory once stayed up all night wondering where the sun had gone. Then it dawned on them.

59 BEANOTOWN TOP-SECRET EXTRATERRESTRIAL RESEARCH STATION (AND TOURIST INFORMATION OFFICE)

The one-stop shop for tourists wanting to know all about Beanotown. And for scientists wondering what ET stands for (their current theory is that it might be something to do with a sore bottom).

GREETINGS FROM PLANET PLOP

TOP SECRET

AREA 51

CINEMA

POOL

WIDL

60 ST SOMEWHERE

Tired of having insomnia? Not got the faintest idea why you passed out? It sounds like you need to visit St Somewhere hospital.

61 BEANOTOWN SWIMMING POOL

Now filled with actual water, the Beanotown swimming pool is the perfect place to practise your butterfly stroke, diving skills and verruca-plaster dodging skills.

Squelchology

Part 6

A DEAD-MYSTERIOUS LITTLE SQUELCHY THING

Where the Dead-mysterious Little Squelchy Thing comes from, nobody knows. Where the Dead-mysterious Little Squelchy Thing is going, nobody knows. That's because it's mysterious (the clue's in the name). What we do know is that this shifty-looking character likes big hats and even bigger moustaches. Oh, and making squelchy sounds.

SHIFTY LURKINGS!

A DAFT LITTLE BOUNCING SQUELCHY THING

BOING!

BOING! SQUELCH!

With more bounces than a barrel of balls dropped from a tall building, you'll probably hear the Daft Little Bouncing Squelchy Thing before you see it. Listen out for the distinctive 'boing squelch boing squelch boing squelch boing squelch' sound, then look up to check if it's going to land on your head. If it does, you'll look like you're wearing a big squashy wig.

A GLUTTONOUS LITTLE SQUELCHY THING

GUZZLE! GORGE! STUFF!

CRAM!

Squelchier than a giant beach ball rammed full of baked-bean juice, the Gluttonous Little Squelchy Thing loves to cram as much food as he can into his gaping, quivering guzzle-hole (mouth).

Nobody can be sure how this wobbly little munchbag came to be so blubbersome. All we know for sure is that if you lick his tummy, it tastes like chutney. And afterwards you'll never, ever want to eat chutney again.

A LITTLE SQUELCHY THING THAT GOES 'NEEP-NEEP!'

NEEP-NEEP!

Why does this particular Squelchy Thing go 'neep-neep!'? We may never know, but we can wildly speculate. I think it's either imitating a car horn (it likes angry drivers) or it's trying to do an impression of a cow and is confused about how cows sound. Yep, I'm sure it's definitely one of those. If it's not, I'll tear up my plummeting license (don't worry, plummeting fans – I have a spare one at home).

What's on at the BEANOTOWN RiTZY?

All the magic of Hollywood, right here in Beanotown!

MUTiNY ON THE BOUNCY CASTLE

Historical drama about two sailors who get into a furious argument when they both go on a bouncy castle at the same time.

KiNG CORN

Exciting adventure film about a mysterious island that is home to a 150-foot-tall cob of corn. A very **angry** cob of corn . . .

iRONiNG MAN

Suspenseful thriller about a man ironing his laundry. Will he ever manage to get his shirt collars wrinkle free?

SPEND A NIGHT UNDER THE STARS* AT

BEANOTOWN CAMPSITE!

Here at the Beanotown Campsite we offer our guests a truly in-tents outdoor experience.

SUMMER SPECIAL
All the mosquitoes you can feed!

*If your tent gets stolen.

YOU MUST BE... JOE KING!

Why are movie stars so cool?

Because they have loads of fans!

139

MEET THE LOCALS

ERIC/BANANAMAN

Banaman has the power to look only *slightly* silly when wearing a blue leotard.

NAME: Eric Wimp, aka Bananaman. (SHHH! Don't tell anyone!)

ADDRESS: 29 Acacia Road.

FAVOURITE COLOUR: Yellow, of course.

FEATHERED SIDEKICK: Crow.

ALL ABOUT ERIC

To the residents of Acacia Road, Eric Wimp seems like nothing more than an incredibly average schoolboy with slightly odd hair. But Eric leads an exciting double life: when he eats a banana, he turns into a heroic crime-fighter (and alien-fighter and all-round baddie-fighter) known as BANANAMAN. Ever alert for the call to action, the fruit-fuelled hero is here to protect the Earth from an array of villains, evil-doers and the not-very-nice.

BANANAFACTS!

Bananaman has the muscles of twenty men, and the brains of twenty mussels.

Bananaman gets stronger when he eats a banana, but if he eats too many at once he'll get fat and might split his Bananapants™.

Bananaman has a helium-boosted heat finger, so he gets invited to a lot of barbecues in the summer, when people struggle to light the coal.

Bananaman can soar like a bird. He also gets sore if he flies into a building and hits his head.

BANANAMAN'S TOP BANANA GADGETS

Thermal Banana

Banana Laser Gun (for blowing up enemies)

Bananakerchief (for blowing his nose)

Electronic Thermal Underwear (it gets cold in space)

Banana Bike (it's Eric's normal bike, but it's much better for the environment than a Bananacar)

KNOW YOUR ENEMY!

BANANAMAN HAS A NUMBER OF ENEMIES TO WATCH OUT FOR. STUDY THEM AND MEMORIZE THEIR WICKED FACES, IN CASE THEY POP UP IN YOUR TOWN.

GENERAL BLIGHT

Bananaman's arch-enemy, General Blight, has a nose for trouble (it's a very big nose) and is always plotting to take over the world. If only he were as clever as he is villainous, he would probably succeed.

AUNTIE

General Blight's hitlady. Don't be fooled into thinking that Auntie is just a harmless old biddy. She is armed with deadly remote-controlled balls of knitting wool, and an incredibly long and really boring story about going to the shops to buy milk that will put you to sleep within minutes.

APPLEMAN

Thoroughly evil to the core, Appleman is in no way ap-peel-ing. In fact, he's a deeply rotten sort who pips the rest of the villains to . . . (OK, OK, that's more than enough apple jokes — Ed.)

KING ZORG

The leader of the Nerks, King Zorg is an alien who intends to conquer Earth at any cost. Preferably at a cost of less than £5 though, because the exchange rate between British pounds and Nerkonian dollars is really high and it's costing him a fortune to run his fleet of Nerk starships.

FROM A FRIEND

FAZZOW!

DOCTOR GLOOM

Blight's sidekick, mad scientist Doctor Gloom is the moustached merchant of malice, the despicable doctor of dastardliness, the hairy-lipped harbinger of horrible, the . . . well, you get the idea.

EDDIE THE GENT

The leader of the Heavy Mob, Eddie the Gent seems like a dapper, well-mannered English gentleman. But don't be fooled, for Eddie will try to steal anything. He often carries a bar of soap around with him, as he likes to make a clean getaway.

MAZOOF!

CROW FACT FILE

Some call him Crow, some call him the Winged Wonder, others the Corvid Crusader. Crow is Eric's best friend and provides Bananaman with the fruity fuel he needs to save the world.

Crow is the real brains behind Bananaman, helping the blue bungler with useful advice, like reminding him how to fly and how doors work. In fact, he's had to help Bananaman out so much that we've made a list about it.

FOUR THINGS CROW HAS HAD TO REMIND BANANAMAN ABOUT

Not to fly through ceilings (this is a very expensive way of leaving a building).

Light switches (Bananaman kept asking why the sun had gone out indoors).

Keeping his secret identity, er, secret. Chief O'Reilly was starting to get suspicious. Either that, or he had indigestion.

How big a wally he is sometimes. This doesn't serve any practical purpose, but Crow likes to have a quip handy when he's run out of actual advice.

Beanotown Classifieds

HAVE YOU SEEN MY KEYS? I've lost them again, but they are always in the last place you look. I need some other places to look first.
Call 0141 496 0979

HUGE HANDS FOR HIRE. Can't open a jam jar? Need some furniture lifed? Call Mrs Bea Feehands today on 0808 1 57 0000

THERE'S NOTHING LIKE A NICE PLATE OF SAUSAGES. And this is nothing like a nice plate of sausages – it's a golfing umbrella. £25 or nearest offer. 029 2018 0349

LOOKING FOR A BARGAIN? Then don't bother reading the rest of this advert. I've got a tatty old dictionary with loads of pages missing and I want a million pounds for it. 020 946 0279

FOR SALE: TIME MACHINE. Quick sale wanted for working time machine. I went back in time and got chased by a dinosaur. Plus, hamburgers hadn't been invented yet. It was awful. Call 0141 496 0979

FREE DOG FOR A GOOD HOME. My dog isn't very good – it never comes when I call it and it doesn't want to play fetch. Plus it has wings and lays eggs. Weird? 029 2018 0349

WHOOPEE CUSHION FOR SALE. Hardly used, only sat on a few times. Plenty of good trumps left in it. £2 or nearest offer. Call 0141 496 0979

USED GRAVESTONE. Ideal for anyone called Bertie McClumclum who died this year at the age of 78. £25 or nearest offer. 029 2018 0321.

SANDWICH FOR SALE. Cheese and pickle sandwich, less than a week old. I bought it then remembered I'm allergic to cheese. Pickle may have been licked off. £5. Call 020 346 0239

BURGLAR WANTED. Are you good at breaking into houses and stealing stuff that isn't yours? The police would like to speak to you. Pop down to the station any time for a chat, or call 999 and reserve a table in the interview room!

ENVIRONMENTALLY FRIENDLY CAR FOR SALE. Do you care about the planet? Then you'll want to buy this environmentally friendly car. It looks like a bike. £500. Call 0118 496 0000.

SPIDER UNDER MY BED. There's a big hairy spider under my bed and I'm scared. It's free if you want it (collection only). Call 0115 496 0000.

DID YOU THROW A TOMATO AT ME? It really hurt and left a big stain on my shirt. Give me a call and we can ketchup. 0141 496 0499

SOFA FOR SALE. Brand-new, hardly used sofa for sale. It is on fire though, so you'll have to deal with that yourself. Call 029 2018 0000 today, before all that's left is a pile of ashes

HELP WANTED. I've been locked in the Puffin Books office for three weeks now and they don't have a phone. This is the only way I can communicate with the outside world. Send help immediately!

BREAKING NEWS: EVERYTHING IS BROKE
BOY IN RED-AND-BLACK JUMPER SUSPECTE

Squelchology

Part 7

A LITTLE ACCIDENT-PRONE SQUELCHY THING

Throb! Ouch! SQUELCH! The poor Little Accident-prone Squelchy Thing is always getting into scrapes and hurting itself. The Little Accident-prone Squelchy Thing is now so used to wearing bandages that it has taken up a part-time job as a professional Egyptian mummy impersonator.

THROB! BLITHER!

A LITTLE SQUELCHY THING WITH THE WINDY-POPS

BELCH! BAARP!

The result of glugging sloshloads of fizzy drinks far too quickly, the Little Squelchy Thing with the Windy-Pops burps and belches its way around Beanotown. The only cure is to make it drink a glass of water while standing on its head, but so far it's been impossible to tell which end is its head and which end is its bottom. I propose a controlled scientific experiment involving several cans of beans and a sealed room, but I'm yet to obtain the funding.

WINDY BEANS

146

A LITTLE SQUELCHY THING WITH A VERY SILLY HAT

Wearing a hat that's bigger than your own body is not something I would advise under normal circumstances, but the Little Squelchy Thing with a Very Silly Hat has evolved to do it perfectly. As an added bonus, if it ever gets tired it can always turn the hat upside down and go to sleep in it. That does lead to a rather squirmy, slithery hat though.

A LITTLE SQUELCHY THING WITH AN EVEN SILLIER HAT

You thought that last hat was silly? WELL, JUST CHECK OUT THIS LI'L BABY. The hat worn by the Little Squelchy Thing with an Even Sillier Hat is so silly that it should come with a government silliness warning. It's so silly that it deserves an entirely new word to describe how silly it is. I propose 'plopsome'. Please let me know if you come up with any better suggestions.

Out on the TOWN

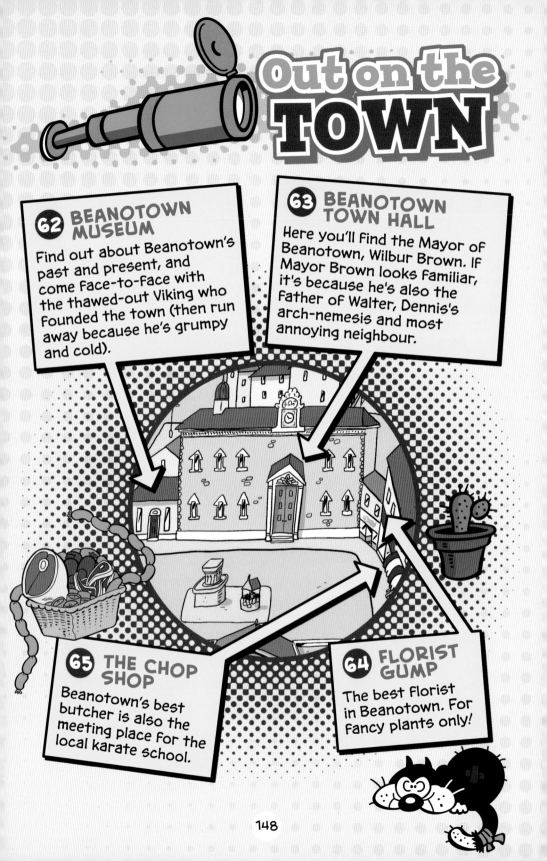

62 BEANOTOWN MUSEUM

Find out about Beanotown's past and present, and come face-to-face with the thawed-out Viking who founded the town (then run away because he's grumpy and cold).

63 BEANOTOWN TOWN HALL

Here you'll find the Mayor of Beanotown, Wilbur Brown. If Mayor Brown looks familiar, it's because he's also the father of Walter, Dennis's arch-nemesis and most annoying neighbour.

65 THE CHOP SHOP

Beanotown's best butcher is also the meeting place for the local karate school.

64 FLORIST GUMP

The best florist in Beanotown. For fancy plants only!

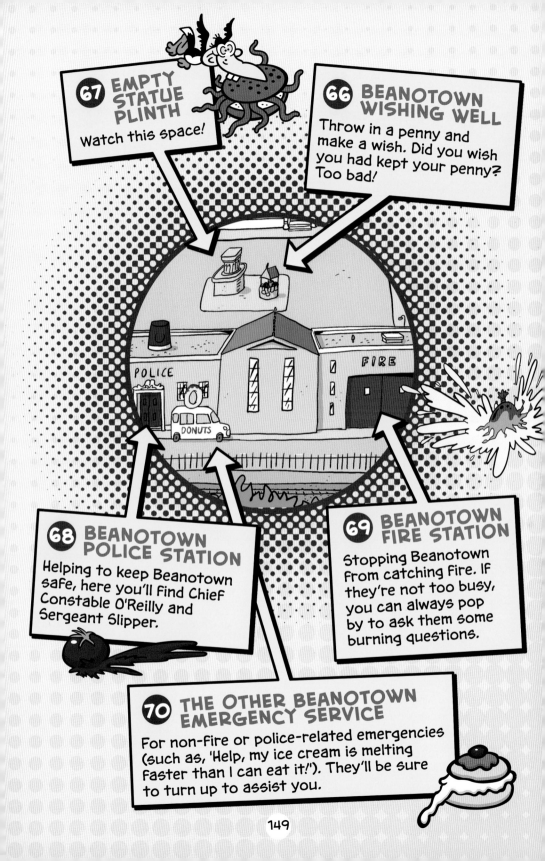

67 EMPTY STATUE PLINTH

Watch this space!

66 BEANOTOWN WISHING WELL

Throw in a penny and make a wish. Did you wish you had kept your penny? Too bad!

68 BEANOTOWN POLICE STATION

Helping to keep Beanotown safe, here you'll find Chief Constable O'Reilly and Sergeant Slipper.

69 BEANOTOWN FIRE STATION

Stopping Beanotown from catching fire. If they're not too busy, you can always pop by to ask them some burning questions.

70 THE OTHER BEANOTOWN EMERGENCY SERVICE

For non-fire or police-related emergencies (such as, 'Help, my ice cream is melting faster than I can eat it!'). They'll be sure to turn up to assist you.

MEET THE LOCALS

NUMBER 13

BORIS
When Boris was little, his parents used to take him to a day-scare centre.

DAD
Once, in the winter, Dad gave someone frostbite, which really made his victim cross.

FRIGHTFUL FACTS!

☠ If you don't keep up regular payments on a ghost, it'll get repossessed.

☠ The wheels on haunted bicycles have spooks.

☠ Vampires find it difficult to get a good night's sleep, because of all the coffin.

☠ Before Mum and Dad got married, she was his ghoulfriend.

MUM
Mum once took up sailing as a hobby – her favourite boat is a blood vessel.

GRAN

Gran doesn't use her broomstick when she's angry (she doesn't want to fly off the handle).

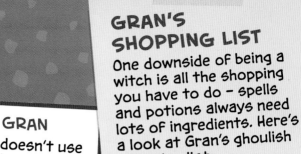

GRAN'S SHOPPING LIST

One downside of being a witch is all the shopping you have to do – spells and potions always need lots of ingredients. Here's a look at Gran's ghoulish shopping list.

- Coven-ready Chips
- Lizard Leg Drumsticks
- Ice Scream
- Fresh Boo-berries
- Scare Spray
- Stake Sandwiches
- Milk (there's nothing spooky about it – it's just that the family needed some).

FRANKIE

Before becoming the butler, Frankie was a musician – he had a monster hit!

TIDDLES

Before they got Tiddles, the family considered getting a dog (a bloodhound).

THE NUMBER 13 GUIDE TO THE PARANORMAL

With so many spooks, monsters and ghouls going around these days, the paranormal can seem like a pretty confusing topic. Here are some useful tips and tricks for dealing with the supernatural!

Remember
Always be very polite around ghosts. Don't spook until you're spooken to.

How To Deal With Werewolves

☠ If you see a werewolf, throw a stick and they'll chase it. Then run away.

☠ If you speak to a werewolf and it doesn't understand you, it must be fur-eign.

☠ If you've got bags of money, a werewolf won't eat you. They don't like rich food.

☠ If a werewolf has a suntan, it's recently been on howl-iday and probably just wants to show you some photos of the beach.

How to Spot a Ghost the Easy Way

Sniff the ghost. Does it smell nice?

YES It's probably just a freshly laundered sheet hanging up on the washing line.

NO It's definitely a ghost.

Are You Frankenstein's Monster?

It can be quite tricky Knowing if you are Frankenstein's monster. Here are some questions you can ask yourself to find out.

- Do you have metal bolts in your neck?

- Do you feel dead on your feet?

- Does your body have more stitches in it than the clothes you're wearing?

- Do people use your big flat head as a shelf to put books on?

- Do you have a screw loose?

If you answered 'yes' to any or all of these questions then you are probably Frankenstein's monster. Sorry!

MEET THE LOCALS

LITTLE PLUM

NAME: Little Plum, aka Little Plum-Stealing Varmint.

AGE: 10

PETS: Treaclefoot the horse.

FAVOURITE CHEESE: Buffalo mozzarella.

Little Plum likes to wear moccasins, as he believes they are good for his sole.

154

ALL ABOUT LITTLE PLUM

Little Plum is a member of the Smellyfeet tribe, along with Chiefy, Pimple and Hole-in-um-Head. Little Plum would like to be a valuable, well-respected member of the Smellyfeet tribe, but something always seems to go wrong.

LEARN TO TRACK, THE SMELLYFEET WAY

Following the tracks of animals and humans is an essential Smellyfeet skill. Look out for the following and one day you can be as good at tracking as Chiefy!

A penguin, on holiday from the South Pole. The Smellyfeet reservation is a popular holiday destination!

A man, walking.

A horse.

A man, running away from a snake.

A horse on a bicycle (stopped to ask for directions).

YOU MUST BE... JOE KING!

What do you call a cowboy who helps out in a school?

The deputy head!

155

THE THREE BEARS

A bear that's been caught in the rain is called a drizzly bear.

NAMES: Pa Bear, Ma Bear and Teddy Bear.

FAVOURITE TIME OF THE YEAR: Hibernation (it's the world's longest lie-in!).

LIKE: All the food at Hank Huckleberry's store.

HATE: The bad end of Hank Huckleberry's blunderbuss.

HOME: This lovely cave!

Our home. Paws off!

156

ALL ABOUT THE THREE BEARS

Pa, Ma and Ted all live in a cave overlooking Greedy Gulch. Unlike the three bears you might have heard of before, there's no way this greedy trio would leave their porridge unguarded - they'd have guzzled it all down as soon as it hit the bowl.

They may not be the smartest bears in the Gulch (Ted is the one with brains) but Pa will always have a pie-pinching plan that he needs help with.

Ted's braces stop his trousers from falling down and showing us his bear bum.

Squelchology

Part 8

MEGA STINK BOMB

A LITTLE SQUELCHY THING WITH APPALLING TASTE IN NECKWEAR

When it comes to fashion, this Little Squelchy Thing is still trapped in the 1970s, a time when ties were massive and featured designs that made you feel a little bit ill. Luckily, the Squelchy Thing with Appalling Taste in Neckwear avoids feeling ill by never looking at itself in a mirror. On the downside, its tie is so big that it trips over it a lot.

A LITTLE SQUELCHY THING WITH A LISP

THQUELCH! THQUELCH!

This Squelchy Thing is easily identified by its lisp. Unfortunately, it sputters its squelches, or should I say 'thquelches'. The best thing to do when you see one is to be polite and never ask it to say, 'Thomas and Nicholas like sausages and sunglasses' – because then it might start crying.

OINK!
BLEAT!
CLUCK!
MOOO!

A VERY CONFUSED LITTLE SQUELCHY THING

This particular Squelchy Thing gets very confused about what it actually is, making it one of the few species that doesn't squelch. Instead, it moos like a cow, baas like a sheep, oinks like a pig and aaaaaahhhhs like a man who has just accidentally hit his thumb with a hammer. Remember, the next time you hear what you think is a familiar animal in the distance, it could easily be the Very Confused Little Squelchy Thing.

A VERY CHEEKY LITTLE SQUELCHY THING

Last in our list is the Very Cheeky Little Squelchy Thing. It's not just last, but also bottom, on account of its big wobbly bum-cheeks. But just because it sticks its bottom out, does that make it rude? It's hard to tell, but I wouldn't want to invite it over for tea in case it dragged its jiggly behind all over the scones.

EVIL LEER!

Well, I hope that I've been helpful and you've learned lots about Squelchology and all the Squelchy Things. Now, if you'll excuse me, I need to find a table to throw myself off. Bye!

Professor Alexander Lemming, SqD

Out on the TOWN

79 BEANOTOWN BRIDGE
Originally there was a plan to build a Beanotown tunnel, but the council didn't dig it.

71 COSTA BUNDLE COFFEE SHOP
The coffee here tastes like mud because it was ground minutes before.

MEGA STINK BOMB

72 BEANOTOWN RAILWAY STATION
Trains to Beanotown-on-Sea leave on the hour. BUT WHY ARE YOU LEAVING?

BEANOTOWN

FACT!
The Beanotown Bubblegum Factory was originally next to the train station, but had to move because all the trains kept saying 'chew chew chew'.

73 TREE
Has the wrong kind of leaves.

77 BEANOTOWN-ON-SEA
A terrific seaside town, though the beach needs some serious kelp. It's now safe to swim here, after the man-eating shark was found not gill-ty.

78 BEANOLAND
Voted 'Best Theme Park Within a Five Minute Drive of Beanotown', Beanoland offers thrills, spills and hopefully no serious accidents since lunchtime!

76 BEANOTOWN LIGHTHOUSE
It can be a lonely job, working at the Beanotown lighthouse. There's nobody to talk to and the sea says nothing – it just waves.

74 SMUGGLERS' CAVES
Used for storing loot in the olden days. Now used for storing water (at high tide).

75 SECRET LOCATION OF BURIED PIRATE TREASURE
Don't tell anyone. It's a secret!

VERY HEAVY WEIGHT INDEED

THE MENACE TEST

Do you think you're as big a Menace as Dennis? Take this test to find out whether you are truly Menace-worthy, or a big Softy instead.

STUCK-UP SQUELCH!

1. WHO LIVES IN BUNKERTON CASTLE?
A) FRANKENSTEIN
B) LORD SNOOTY
C) THE PRIME MINISTER

2. WHAT WAS THE NAME OF THE TRIBE CHASED OUT OF OLD BEANOTOWN BY SOME MENACING VIKINGS?
A) SOFTANS
B) WIMPLINGS
C) FLUFFKINS

3. WHO LIVES WITH DENNIS'S GRAN?
A) DENNIS
B) GNIPPER
C) ALEXANDER LEMMING

MEGA STINK BOMB

4. WHAT IS DENNIS'S LITTLE SISTER CALLED?
A) BETTY
B) BEA
C) BABS

5. WHAT KIND OF DOG IS GNASHER?
A) TRANSYLVANIAN ROUGH-FURRED HAGGIS TERRIER
B) ALBANIAN STUBBLE-LEGGED SAUSAGE POINTER
C) ABYSSINIAN WIRE-HAIRED TRIPE HOUND

6. WHICH OF THESE IS NOT A PART OF THE MENACE'S STANDARD ARSENAL?
A) CATAPULT
B) EGGS
C) FLUFFY TEDDY

7. WHICH OF THE FOLLOWING IS ALEXANDER LEMMMING NOT A PROFESSOR OF?
A) WOBBLEOLOGY
B) SQUIDGETRONOMY
C) SQUISHONOMICS

A LEMMING'S GUIDE TO FIXING FRACTURED FIZZOGS

8. WHAT IS THE NAME OF WALTER'S PET POODLE?
A) FOO FOO
B) WOO WOO
C) POO POO

9. WHAT IS BEANOTOWN'S HOSPITAL CALLED?
A) ST BIFFO
B) ST SOMEWHERE
C) ST FIGARO

10. CALAMITY JAMES'S JUMPER IS . . .
A) BLUE WITH A NUMBER 13
B) RED WITH A NUMBER 7
C) RED WITH A NUMBER 13

11. WHERE DOES LITTLE SCOTTISH SQUELCHY THING COME FROM?

A) SQUASH NESS
B) THE WOBBLY HIGHLANDS
C) BEN WIBBLE

OCH! SEE YOU, SQUELCHY!

12. WHO PLAYS THEIR HOME MATCHES AT COLD TRAFFORD?

A) MENACE ATHLETIC
B) BEANOTOWN ROVERS
C) BEANOTOWN UNITED

13. WHAT IS DONALD SCRIMP'S REALITY TV SHOW CALLED?

A) YOU'RE SACKED!
B) GET OUT OF MY OFFICE!
C) YOU'LL NEVER WORK AGAIN!

14. WHICH OF THE FOLLOWING IS NOT ONE OF THE NUMSKULLS?

A) CRUNCHER
B) BRAINY
C) SNIFFLES

15. WHO IS THE FASTEST BOY IN BEANOTOWN?

A) JACK SWIFT
B) LIGHTNING TODD
C) BILLY WHIZZ

ZOOM!

16. WHO HAS A CAT CALLED WINSTON?

A) JANITOR
B) OLIVE
C) TEACHER

17. WHAT HAPPENED TO BUNKERTON VILLAGE?

A) THE ENTIRE VILLAGE WAS ABDUCTED BY ALIENS
B) LORD SNOOTY HAD IT DESTROYED
C) IT WAS INVADED BY A YETI

18. WHICH OF THESE TWO BASH STREET KIDS ARE RELATED?

A) SIDNEY AND TOOTS
B) WILFRED AND 'ERBERT
C) SPOTTY AND SMIFFY

19. WHO LIVES AT 29 ACACIA ROAD?

A) MINNIE THE MINX
B) CUTHBERT CRINGEWORTHY
C) ERIC WIMP

20. THE THREE BEARS LIVE IN A CAVE OVERLOOKING . . .

A) GREEDY GULCH
B) ROTTEN RAVINE
C) BUM CANYON

ANSWERS

1. B) LORD SNOOTY
2. A) SOFTANS
3. B) GNIPPER
4. B) BEA
5. C) ABYSSINIAN WIRE-HAIRED TRIPE HOUND
6. C) FLUFFY TEDDY
7. C) SQUISHONOMICS (HE SLEPT IN AND MISSED THE EXAM)
8. A) FOO FOO
9. B) ST SOMEWHERE
10. C) RED WITH A NUMBER 13

11. B) THE WOBBLY HIGHLANDS
12. C) BEANOTOWN UNITED
13. A) YOU'RE SACKED!
14. C) SNIFFLES
15. C) BILLY WHIZZ
16. A) JANITOR
17. B) LORD SNOOTY HAD IT DESTROYED (BECAUSE IT WAS SPOILING HIS VIEW)
18. A) SIDNEY AND TOOTS (THEY'RE BROTHER AND SISTER)
19. C) ERIC WIMP
20. A) GREEDY GULCH

HOW DID YOU DO?

16-20 CORRECT ANSWERS

YOU'RE A MIGHTY MENACE! DENNIS HIMSELF WOULD BE PROUD, AND MAYBE EVEN LET YOU BORROW HIS FAVOURITE CATAPULT.

10-15 CORRECT ANSWERS

NOT BAD AT ALL! YOU COULD EASILY SURVIVE A NIGHT IN BEANOTOWN (AS LONG AS YOU DIDN'T STRAY TOO NEAR TO THE YETI, OBVIOUSLY).

4-9 CORRECT ANSWERS

YOU HAVE MUCH TO LEARN. QUICK! ASK CUTHBERT CRINGEWORTHY IF YOU CAN TAKE A LOOK AT HIS HOMEWORK, AND YOU'LL BE A BEANO EXPERT IN NO TIME.

1-3 CORRECT ANSWERS

PAAAARP! PAAAAAAAAARP! RUBBISH ANSWERS ALERT! YOU'RE EITHER A SOFTY OR YOU'RE SECRETLY A GROWN-UP! EITHER WAY, THERE'S DEFINITELY NO HELPING YOU. IT'S THE FIRST TRAIN TO NUTTYTOWN FOR YOU!